Toddler

to

Teen

Mel Hayde

Toddler to Teen

A Positive and Practical Parenting Guide

How to Equip, Encourage and Enjoy Your Children

1st Printing July 2017

2nd Printing October 2017

3rd Printing February 2018

ISBN 978-1-920711-02-3

Copyright ©2017

by Mel Hayde M.Ed., M.Co., M.Th.

All rights reserved. No portion of this publication may be reproduced, stored in a retrieval system or transmitted in any form, by any means – electronic, mechanical, photocopy, recorded or otherwise – without prior written permission of the publisher.

Published by Toddler to Teen, Sydney, Australia.

ABN: 3538 4844 989

Enquiries: melishayde@gmail.com

Blog: www.wordpress.melhayde.com

Printed in Australia by Ingram Sparks.

www.ingramspark.com

Thanks

My greatest thanks is to my Jesus. He is always kind and always good and I am overwhelmingly thankful for the gift of knowing, loving and serving Him, and for the joy and certain hope of eternity with Him.

Thank you also to my precious ones, Caleb (and Kim), Emily (and Simon), and Samuel. It has (mostly) been a delight to equip you for adulthood, to encourage you towards the right way and to enjoy you in each season. You are a wonderful gift from God and I have been challenged, changed and blessed by having you in my life.

I am overwhelmingly thankful for the treasured gift of my friendship with Alison. She has a beautiful heart that is God-centred, others-focused and full of laughter. You have encouraged and supported me so faithfully.

A huge thank you to James and Simone, authors of *Cyber Parenting,* who have provided an excerpt from their book for a chapter, and who generously assisted with the technical aspects of putting this book together.

A special thank you to Andy, Geoff and Peter for their contribution to the Dad-to-Dad chapter. They are men of integrity and kindness who love their wives with gentleness and who lead their children with humour, patience and wisdom.

It has been a privilege to be part of the GFA community for almost 20 years. Thank you for your kindness, fun, generosity and helpful contributions.

Thanks also to Jen for her typing efficiency, Alicia and Melinda for their expert editing, Jon and John for technical assistance, and to Kathryn and Andrew for providing a peaceful location for the writing.

Introduction

I love toddlers. They melt my heart. They are fully immersed in the moment with not a care about what went before or what comes next. They are busy and inquisitive. I love watching them explore their world and discover new things. I so enjoy seeing their unique personality emerge and their interests develop. They are learning words and phrases each day and they love so freely. They are a delight.

I have been speaking and answering questions about toddlers for over 20 years now. I have sold nearly 20 000 copies of the Terrific Toddler books. Parents love their children and want to parent them well. Over the last five years I have had many people ask, 'When are you writing a book about teens?' This book has combined a revised and updated version of *Terrific Toddlers* and *Terrific Toddlers Two* into one book.

Each chapter has additional sections on how that concept applies to the school aged years (5 to 12-year-olds) and then to the teenage years (13-years-old and up). Scattered throughout the book are testimonies from real families who have implemented these principles with their toddlers and have reaped the fruit of that early training in the later years. It also contains the valuable addition of a chapter on cyber parenting in this digital age.

My prayer is that you will be convicted about the importance of parenting. To train little hearts up in the right way is a high calling. It takes commitment, sacrifice, and oh, so much time. It is frustrating, challenging and exhausting. It is also satisfying, rewarding and exhilarating. I trust that this little book will help you to help them live well and love well.

Contents

1	A Picture Story	8
2	Positive Parenting	10
3	Managing Anger	17
4	Some Basics	25
5	The Root Cause	31
6	Benefits for Parents	38
7	Benefits for your Child	41
8	Balancing Acts	45
9	Flexibility	50
10	Daily Activities – One	54
11	Daily Activities – Two	67
12	Motivating Behaviour	87
13	Implementation	93
14	More than One	100
15	Parental Model	104
16	Daily Life	108
17	Self-Control	111
18	Obedience	115
19	Speech	124
20	Kindness	129
21	Patience	133
22	Friendship	138
23	Helpfulness	146
24	Cheerfulness	151
25	Fun	157
26	Bumps Along the Way	160
27	Cyber-Parenting	162
28	Dad to Dad	169
29	How the Story Ends	175
30	Questions	180
Resources		207

1

A Picture Story

You are very, very pleased with yourself. About 18 months ago you moved into a brand-new house. Everything was beautiful, fresh and modern. You have greatly enjoyed every aspect of your new house and feel very comfortable there. Of course, there has been the odd little thing that has needed attention, but generally everything has been working fine.

Just recently, however, you have noticed a few wet, sticky, smelly brown patches appearing on the pristine white carpet of your lounge room floor. A month or two ago you had just one or two a day and you were able to clean them up fairly well. However, now they are regularly appearing 10 to 20 times a day.

They seem to be wetter, stickier, smellier and 'browner'. Cleaning them up is taking up a lot of your time, and you are feeling quite frustrated by this. You are also a little embarrassed. When friends come to visit, they can't help but notice your floor.

Luckily, three people come to your door offering to help you with this problem.

The first man tells you not to worry about them, that everyone has them, just endure them and they will eventually go away. He also tells you they will probably reappear when the house is about 13 years old and stay for 5 – 6 years before finally disappearing for good.

The second man tells you that everyone has them, and yes, they are embarrassing, but he shows you how to clean them up each time they appear.

Yes, that takes up a lot of your day and it isn't very pleasant, but the patches are removed for a few hours and the lounge room looks fairly tidy, temporarily.

The third man tells you that you don't have to have wet, sticky, smelly brown patches in your house at all. He will show you how to work on the causes of the problem and how to clean the patches up so that they will not reappear.

He can also show you how to avoid encountering them in your next house. The only catch is that your current lounge room will actually look much worse for a month or two, before the patches are removed for good.

Which man's advice will you follow?

The wet, sticky, smelly brown patches on the carpet can be likened to the problem behaviours that generally emerge in children around 18 months of age and last for two years or more.

Some books will tell you just to endure these behaviours, other books will tell you how to react to each problem as it appears. My hope is that this book will help you understand the root of these problems so you can be a positive, proactive parent and avoid most of these unpleasant behaviours altogether.

The foundation you lay in the early years will give you a strong platform from which to journey through the school and teen years too.

2

Positive Parenting

As parents, we quite naturally work towards suppressing the frustrating, annoying and embarrassing traits we see developing in our children. However, by focusing on the positive, parents can enjoy the training process and their child will thrive in that environment too.

Looking back, I can say that about 90% of my training was positive and encouraging, with the rest being negative and corrective. I always tried to say three positive comments to every negative one, and that was quite difficult on some days.

Remember that you have eighteen years of parenting so you can afford to work on one or two behaviours at a time. You don't need to achieve it all today.

Make your first contact in the morning special. A hug, a special hello, or a simple, 'I love you' sets a lovely tone for the day. Always speak politely and kindly to your child, as so much of how your child will interact with their siblings and others depends on your model.

Speak with a happy and excited voice about the plan for the day or the new event. Children will usually follow our lead, eventually. Praise your child for making good choices, particularly after a time of testing. As a 15-month-old Emily was quite determined to touch the video recorder and I had to teach her that she could not. At times, you could actually 'see' her little mind work as she would walk towards the video, put her little hand out and then bring it back in, turn around and find her toys! I would go overboard with the praise at this point, with lots of clapping and cheering, and more and more often she would choose to play with her own toys rather than the video player due to the positive reaction she received.

Praise them when they:
- are playing with toys (not 'non-toy' items)
- share a toy with another child
- ask for a drink in a happy (not whiny) voice
- say hello politely to a visitor
- have their hair washed without screaming
- demonstrate self-control

Children love praise and they need it.

Present your instructions in a positive, rather than negative, light. For example, replace 'Don't hit' with 'Be kind'. If you have more than one child you can direct a positive comment to one, rather than a negative comment to the other. For example, at the table, I would direct a compliment to the child who had remembered to sit still with their hands in their lap for their beautiful manners, and almost 99% of the time the other (who had not) followed.

I loved being at home with my children when they were small and we made up lots of fun rhymes and songs that say 'I love you' (which I won't share with you). Focus on teaching your child all the positive attributes you desire to see in their little hearts. Virtues of kindness, honesty, compassion, love, gentleness, patience, integrity, perseverance, hospitality, politeness, goodness, friendship and cheerfulness are all a delight to teach to your child.

Write a list and then creatively teach them into your day. As you work on a chore together, talk about doing it for the rest of the family with a cheerful heart. Read stories displaying positive virtues, colour-in pictures of children sharing, display gentleness when caring for the family pet and make up games and stories filled with fun and wise words.

Incorporate positive teaching into all of your everyday activities. This is fun and challenging for you and gives great significance to those cyclic tasks you have each day. It also ensures your toddler is receiving mostly positive words and instructions in their day too.

As a parent, you set the tone for the whole household. If your entire day was recorded on tape, would it be characterised by negative or positive comments? Is your home peaceful and fun? Do you enjoy being there? Do your children?

School Years

During this season, it is important to continue to speak encouraging and positive words to your children. Words such as 'You are a cheerful helper', and 'Thanks for helping your younger brother fix that puzzle piece' and 'I'm so glad you are in our family' are creating an environment of acceptance and affirmation. A home filled with life-giving words is peaceful and pleasant.

It is important not to praise your child for every task they perform. At this stage, they should just be completing their personal responsibilities without the need of acknowledgement and praise. In the classroom, the teacher will not be commenting on every correct decision, and children who are expecting this can be discouraged. Encourage your child to do right because it is right and focus your words on the positive character traits you observe.

Also, do avoid empty praise or flattery. Every drawing they show you does not need to be declared a masterpiece. Scoring a goal in a sports game does not require predictions of future success as a professional sportsman. Children cannot be whatever they want. There are limitations. It is kind and honest to help them realise that they will have strengths and weaknesses and to keep their achievements in perspective.

Teen Years

During this stage, your teen is becoming a unique individual. They will be different to you. They will like music you don't even understand. They will dress in combinations you would never dream of wearing. They will make choices with their time and money that baffle you. They will begin to form their own viewpoints on wider issues and world events.

Most obviously, they are digital natives, born into a world of technology that wasn't even around when you were born. This impacts the way they relate to their friends, how they study and learn, how they interact with the world and how they organise social functions. It can be confusing, frustrating and challenging.

Being a positive parent in this stage requires careful thought. Is an extreme haircut with bright colours worthy of dispute and strife? Is the combination of baggy shorts and a mismatched T-shirt worthy of a battle of words and scorn? Do you constantly nag over the upcoming assignment or do you allow your teen to experience the logical consequence from the school for not handing it in on time? This valuable lesson learned here has far less significant consequences than later at university or in the workplace.

Issues that are not harmful to others, or expensive in terms of time or resources, or ethically questionable can be overlooked. Keep your serious discussions for the big issues and look to build relationship with your teen. One mum was recently sharing that she has a few rap songs on her playlist, thanks to her son introducing her to this genre. She did also mention that she still doesn't like most rap songs!

Endeavour to connect once a week with your teen. A coffee date or a meal out is a great chance to stay connected. Keep the conversation light and focus on mutual topics of interest. Don't be discouraged if your teen doesn't really talk during this time some weeks. That is quite normal. The time together may be quite short some weeks, while in other weeks it will be hard to stop them talking. Just enjoy the talking weeks. It is the pattern of meeting together regularly and speaking words of encouragement and support that will mean so much to your teen.

Proverbs 24:3-4 'By wisdom a house is built, by knowledge the rooms are filled with all precious and pleasant riches.'

Terrific Toddlers has been an invaluable resource for our family and many others whom we have shared it with. The practical, no nonsense advice presented in an easy to read format means that everyone can access this fantastic information. To be honest, when I first read Terrific Toddlers, I was a little overwhelmed - there were so many good ideas and being a pretty flexible person, I felt like there was a lot of structure I would need to somehow incorporate into my day.

So, I started with just one thing. I started by spending 15 minutes with my daughter each morning at the start of her room time. I couldn't believe the difference it made! Her behaviour honestly changed after just a few days. Instead of whining and clinging to me throughout the day, she was happy to play independently for longer and was generally happier. I couldn't believe it!

I figured seeing as that piece of advice had worked so well, I'd implement another and another until I had incorporated all the ideas Mel had shared in Terrific Toddlers. Suddenly the toddler years became a joy for me instead of a stress. I LOVE that Mel addresses the heart of the behaviour and hence the heart of the child. I loved that I could train my children from the inside out because I know that's how lasting, deep character is built. Terrific Toddlers was the perfect map to guide our family through four toddler seasons and we are incredibly grateful to Mel Hayde for putting together such a practical and helpful resource.

Charissa, Mum to 4

I grew up in a Middle Eastern family and when it was time for a toddler to go to bed, it was often the Mother's role to take the toddler to the bedroom and spend about 45 mins with the child in the bed helping them to fall asleep. The issue was that my Mum was, and still is, a great cook, and all the guests that came over knew that. So, by the time these poor Middle Eastern mothers eventually cajoled their child to sleep, all the good food was gone! When I saw that, I told myself... 'There is no way I'm going to allow that to happen in my family, my wife and I are not going to miss out on my Mum's amazing food'.

And we never have! If we were out at my parent's house or at a mate's place, we would spend about 5 min putting our toddlers to bed in a portable cot in a quiet room, make sure they were okay and we were out, ready to enjoy dinner with our family and friends. So, when the kids got older and we were out a bit later than normal, they knew what to do and would find a quiet place on a couch somewhere and rest there while we finished up with the guests.

Our belief has always been that when we are visiting people in their homes, we wanted to train our toddlers to have the self-control to either be able to sit and read/write or play with a few toys while we are visiting. And as they got slightly older and more mature they were better equipped to listen or to engage with friends in a conversation and learn from people's life stories and experiences. The one thing we didn't want was to see our toddlers tearing up someone's home and then not being invited back again. So, we always made a point of making sure our kids took a book or some type of activity (crayons, paper) with them when we went to a friend's home.

Just today as I write this, we went to visit my parents because they had an international visitor who wanted to meet our family. Our kids are now 12, 13, 15 and 17. After we had all greeted my parents and the guest, we sat down in the lounge room and began to chat with him. After about 10 minutes of casual conversation, the guest said that he was surprised that our kids had not pulled out their electronic devices and started playing with them, but rather, either pulled out a book to read or just sat and listened to the conversation. He stated that he had never seen this before.

Claude, Dad to 4

3

Managing Anger

One rainy morning I had one child spill their whole bowl of cereal over the table and another child knock their glass of milk so that it shattered over the floor. I also had two loads of washing left over from the day before, a very grumpy school aged boy, and a toddler who had woken up and decided that today was a 'No' day.

Do you ever have mornings that sound similar?

Many of the mums I have spoken to admit to struggling with frustration that leads to yelling, hitting and even verbal abuse. Some situations seem to test our patience beyond its limit. The depth of feeling a stubborn toddler can arouse is quite startling. The following suggestions may help you minimise these outbursts.

Having a **flexible** pattern for your day is the greatest tool to help you avoid many, many situations that are typically frustrating during the toddler years. You will be able to manage your responsibilities and your toddler in a calm and orderly way that will greatly reduce outbursts from you and your toddler.

Look after yourself in terms of nutrition, water intake, exercise and adequate sleep. During the Australian Open Tennis, I stay up too late watching it on TV, and I am a very grumpy mummy for those two weeks! Plan some fun for yourself each day. I love my hour of reading or cross-stitch every afternoon and feel more relaxed afterwards.

Have a hobby or interest outside the children. A craft, sport, or just anything you can look forward to each week. Try and have something that 'grows' each week (for example a craft project) or something that has measurable progress or results. It is a good balance to the cyclic tasks we are responsible for day after day.

Ensure you have time away from being a mum each week. In the early years of my parenting I would meet with friends for breakfast every Saturday. Yes, in my absence my children were dressed in odd combinations (I would call them my rainbow babies!) and sometimes the housework was still waiting to be done when I got back, but the break always lifted my spirits.

When speaking to your child, make sure you have full eye contact to save the frustration of having to repeat your instructions. This is particularly important for boys... big and small.

Respond with proper instruction, the first time your child whines, and not the tenth. Your internal temperature will rise with every repeat.

Attempt to admonish your child in the same place, making an effort to discuss the behaviour in private, never in front of siblings or visitors. This helps prevent the parent from lashing out on the spot. Leave your child in their cot or on their bed until you are calm enough to deal with the behaviour. I had one memorable afternoon where all three needed to be dealt with. I put the older two on a bed each, the toddler in his cot, and sat outside with a diet coke. Fifteen minutes later I was able to go in and calmly deal with them in turn.

Try whispering when you are really mad, it can calm the situation. Talk through situations in times of non-conflict. For example, have your toddler practice packing up their toys quickly when you are not racing out the door. Turn it into a fun game.

As you calmly and consistently respond to your child and the events of your day, your child will also follow your example and this will result in a peaceful home for you all. Most importantly, you are setting an example of how to manage anger and how to communicate well, despite the emotions of the moment.

School Years

One of the biggest triggers for anger in mums during the school years is the getting ready for school process. When my little ones were just starting school, we could hear the neighbour, several houses down, yelling at her children every morning.

If you keep doing what you are doing, you will keep getting what you are getting.

I tried several morning patterns before I found one that worked, but that early effort paid off for the many years that followed. I will outline my morning pattern and hopefully you can adjust this to fit your own family.

The alarm was set for 7:00 am and they had to do the 'before breakfast 1-2-3' of getting dressed, making their bed and tidying their room before breakfast. They made their own breakfast of toast and cereal every weekday morning (special breakfasts were kept for the weekend). After breakfast, they needed to do their 'breakfast 1-2-3' of putting their plates on the sink, cleaning their placemat and then making their own lunch (a sandwich, a snack food, two plain biscuits and a piece of fruit) and put it straight in their bag which was then placed near the door. Then it was time to do the 'after breakfast 1-2-3' of brushing teeth, washing their face and brushing their hair. Then they put on their shoes and socks. For some reason, if they put these on at this point in the morning, it only took two or three minutes. If they put them on just as we were leaving it would take five to ten minutes.

Then they had the freedom to read until it was time to leave for school. We needed to leave the house to walk to school at 8:30 am so I was aiming to have them sitting and reading by 8:00 am. This meant that if they were sitting down by 8:10 am or even 8:20 am, there was no last minute mad scramble and frayed tempers as we aimed to leave on time.

Of course, this did not all happen straight away. At first, each child had a checklist on the fridge and they would tick off each task as they completed it. They earned a small ice cream treat on Friday afternoon for the first few weeks to encourage this new skill. Then they were encouraged to complete the tasks without the checklist and after a few weeks it was just the pattern for the morning. I enjoyed not yelling and they enjoyed not being yelled at.

Teen Years

In the early teen years, you have the tension of your child wanting more freedom than you feel they are ready for. This is a characteristic of this stage of development and can be the cause of much disagreement. It is so natural to feel angry that they are dismissing your great wisdom! I was expecting this time of transition and deliberately planned to model speaking calmly as we discussed these tricky issues.

Caleb asked to ride his bike to the shops. Rather than give an outright no (my first response) I had him write out three reasons I might say yes and three reasons I might say no. We then used his answers as the basis of a discussion for whether he should be allowed to have this new freedom. Taking the time to think it through initially, and then to address the issue at a set time greatly helped me to speak calmly and quietly.

In the later teen years, you have the tricky task of letting them make mistakes and reaping the consequences. One mother was so angry that her child would forget his work shifts and turn up at the wrong times. She tried to nag and yell but her teen was still constantly late. He eventually lost his job. This natural consequence ensured he was more careful with his next job.

Another dad shared that he had spoken to his child over and over about the folly of speeding in his car. The heated discussions were repeated over and over and his son continued to drive recklessly. One day the son was given a hefty fine and a six-month suspension. Two more fines and suspensions later, he now drives within the speed limit. Our anger does not change a teen's behaviour. Our responsibility is to speak truth in a respectful manner and to keep loving them even through their mistakes.

Proverbs 15:1 'A gentle answer turns away wrath, a harsh word stirs up anger.'

One of the main things I am grateful for is training our toddlers to practice folding their hands to help them gain self-control – we called it 'Quiet Hands'. We would train them that when we asked them to fold their hands together they also needed to keep quiet and not talk at all. We trained them to be able to do this for at least 5 minutes.

*This skill has been **so** beneficial during those times when things were getting heated between our 4 kids. Whether it was in the car, visiting a friend or sitting in a meeting, I would look at them and say, 'For the next 5 minutes I want you all to do quiet hands.' And they would do it. (Obviously, we trained them at home previously so they knew that when we asked them to do that we actually meant it). Well let me tell you. . . oh, the peace and quiet that came into that situation when they did it. You could hear yourself think, you could relax and take control of the situation.*

You know what? We still use it . . . although now only on rare occasions, mainly in the car and our kids are 12, 13, 15 and 17. Sometimes when your teens are squabbling and arguing about issues and you can't decide who is right or wrong and you just need silence, 'quiet hands' has been invaluable in bringing quietness, peace and some clarity to a situation.

Lidiya, Mum to 4

Mel has helped me parent with the end in sight. She always told me that we have 18 years to parent. It all doesn't have to be fixed or right straight away! That encouraged me to keep persevering in training my girls, even when I didn't see immediate results/fruit. All along the journey, my two main goals have been for my kids to be morally responsive and that they would be a blessing to everyone they come into contact with.

The road has not been easy. I have two very strong-willed girls and I became a single mum when they were only 7 & 4 years old. But I am so thankful for Mel's books. In particular, I am glad I had a structure to my day and stayed at home most days when the girls were toddlers and preschool age. Learning to obey mum when I said it was room time, playdoh time, book time or outside time has proven to be so helpful long term!

It has meant that when they were in primary school they were a blessing to their teachers because they could obey the teacher's instructions straight away. And now as I'm teaching Jo to drive, I am confident that she will stop when I say stop, without arguing, which is a huge blessing. It has meant that we have been able to have so many fun road trips this year and connect deeply as we chat and sing together, all the while knowing that if I need to instruct or correct Jo, she will be able to accept my correction graciously.

As I write this, Jessica is 20 years old and living out of home. She is working really hard to be responsible for her own rent and other expenses. She is at university and studying well. I am just so proud of her being so responsible. I see that as fruit from the early years of training in being responsible for her own toys and books.

If something breaks you replace it. One time when she was young she borrowed a friend's scooter, and then lost it at the park. It wasn't easy, but I took her to the shops and I made Jess use her savings to buy a new scooter for her friend. It was difficult at the time. Her friends at school certainly wouldn't have been made to do that. I felt like a pretty unkind mum, but now I see the fruit and it is so beautiful. Jessica's character is beautiful. And that was what I was aiming for! For her to be a blessing!

Alison, Mum to 2

4

Some Basics

First, let's just quickly highlight three obvious causes of 'messes', or inappropriate behaviour - nutrition, sleep and clutter.

Nutrition

Toddler Years

Do ensure your toddler is eating healthy meals at regular times. Snack foods, take-away foods, sweets and soft drinks will all have a negative effect on your child's behaviour. Watch the amount of colourings and preservatives your child is consuming, and keep processed foods to a minimum. Make a written note each time your child 'explodes' and see if there is a connection with food.

Regular behaviour 'explosions' after parties or food treats from visitors may be an indication that your child is sensitive to particular foods. Keep take-away food for a rare treat, not a weekly expectation. Have three meals a day and fruit for morning and afternoon teas. Avoid snacking, or grazing all day. Not sure if food is an issue? Try a totally healthy diet for six weeks and observe the differences in your child.

School Years

When I went back to teaching after a ten-year absence to raise my children, I was shocked by the changes to the students' diets. All students were coming out into the playground, for both recess and lunch, with two handfuls of packet food full of colours, preservatives, sugar and fat. It was hard to find a child with a piece of fruit, or just a plain biscuit or a homemade sandwich. Do provide your children with real food for school. They are most capable of making a sandwich with a spread and placing it in a sandwich bag or a lunch container. Have a box of snack food, a bowl of fruit and the plain crackers in easy reach and they can complete their lunch independently. If they refill their water bottle after school each afternoon, then that is easy to pop in their school bag each morning.

Teen Years

The teens at school live on take-away food. They seem to consume it at least five times a week and many are having numerous store-bought coffees in a day too. Some grab a sugar-filled treat for breakfast on the way to school each morning. This affects their ability to concentrate in the classroom and has an impact on their skin, hair and general health too.

Each of my teens went through this phase when they started their part-time jobs and had their own money to spend. After a few weeks (or months) they realised that the money could be spent better elsewhere and they felt better too if these foods were kept for weekend treats rather than everyday food. As the parent, we can model wise choices towards nutrition and hopefully our children will (eventually) follow our positive example.

Sleep

Toddler Years

Toddlers need somewhere between 10 – 14 hours of sleep each day. Do ensure your child has a rest or nap each day and is in bed each night at a reasonable time. So many of the problem toddler questions are often the result of a tired child – too many activities each week (for the child and/or for mum) or irregular night sleep patterns. A well-rested toddler is much more likely to be a happy toddler.

School Years

I sent my children to school for four days a week in the first term of Kindergarten. We had Wednesday at home to rest and play. This greatly helped the transition to big school and I cherished this day at home with them. Also, they were involved in one activity outside school for the infant school years, and two (a sport and a musical instrument) for the primary school years. Too many activities can make them over-tired.

During the school years, it is important to establish good sleep habits. Implement a night time ritual that enables your child to slow down and ready themselves for sleep. The ritual of teeth, toilet, reading, talking and then prayers was consistent each night. Reading for 20 – 30 minutes enables them to still their bodies and their minds and eased the transition to night rest. A solid 10 – 12 hours each night is the best preparation for optimal performance at school.

Teen Years

The teens at school are regularly falling asleep at 2:00 am or 3:00 am each morning. It is not uncommon for them to stay up all night, playing a computer game or engaging on social media. Many of them sleep with their phones under their pillow so they can respond the moment a text or notification comes through. Most do not have a set bedtime. This, of course, greatly minimises their ability to engage well with their learning. They wander through the day half-asleep and they are often irritable and disagreeable too.

If you have set good sleep patterns in the early years, it is much easier to continue these in the teen years. Expecting everyone to be in bed by a certain time each week night as a courtesy to each other is not unreasonable. A later bedtime can be set for Friday and Saturday nights. Technology devices can be placed on the kitchen bench at bedtime so as not to be a distraction. Computer games can be limited to the weekends. You are the parent, you can set the boundaries. A well-rested teen is a much happier teen.

Clutter

Toddler Years

Avoid noise and object clutter in your house. It is very important to ensure you have a reasonably quiet and tidy house to provide the best environment in which your child can live and learn.

Clutter can create distractions and frustrations. It will also create bothersome delays for each of your activities in your day. Mum and toddler will be constantly frustrated if they need to search for crayons and paper or all the parts of a toy before they can begin playing. Have a place for each item and have an orderly system for storing all household objects, especially the toys. You can't organise mess – if you have too much 'stuff' then maybe consider throwing away or giving away the surplus to someone in need.

Excessive noise can also be distracting for your young child. Having a loud television on, a radio blaring and some music all playing in the house at the same time will hinder your toddler's ability to focus and concentrate. Have the television on for selected shows only and keep background music at a low volume.

A calm and orderly environment will particularly help your active toddler manage your instructions and his play tasks.

School Years

This is the season to establish the patterns of orderliness and tidiness. Establish what you will be doing with all the bits of paper your child will be bringing home from school. Are you going to keep everything? If so, how can you store it in a clutter-free manner? Will you keep it in a box and then cull it at the end of the school year? Or will you display it on the fridge for a week and throw it out when the next item comes home?

Encourage your child to pack up after each activity and to have a home for each set of toys. This is setting lifelong habits of orderliness that help reduce stress and aid life-satisfaction and productivity. At the start of each school holidays have your child sort through their toys and clothes and give away what they no longer use or need.

Teen Years

Provide a study area that is free from visual and movement clutter. A desk in a study or their bedroom is preferable to one in the main living area of the house. Provide them with containers and drawers in their colour scheme that will aid organisation. Ensure that there is adequate shelving for their resources. A clutter-free environment is calm and will aid concentration and retention of information.

Most of the teens I teach do not make their beds or wash and iron their own clothes. Giving your teens the responsibility of these things will enhance their appreciation for the effort that goes into producing clean clothes. It will help them to care for their garments and will generally encourage them to put them in cupboards rather than on the floor.

Psalm 37:37 'Consider the blameless, observe the upright; a future awaits those who seek peace.'

> *For me it's the boundaries. Simple I know. Having toddlers learn boundaries and following through all through their training years we have started to see the results. Adelaide (15) now appreciates the boundaries she has had in her life as she is understanding more now why the boundaries were so important. In saying that it's not been without many struggles and tears... both toddler and adolescent! Especially when everyone else was doing things that Adelaide wasn't allowed for that season. Obviously, her boundaries are widening and she is enjoying that but has self-control and is usually 'ready' for the next thing. Boundaries have added to our relationship in that as she has grown older we can talk it through. And at times even thanked us for not giving her freedoms too early. It is much easier to start out with boundaries than try and pull back!*
>
> **Kristy, Mum to 6**

> *The thing I have found the most helpful is teaching my children self-control. I thought it was a good thing to teach my children, but I never realised how helpful it would be - doctor appointments, shopping lines, church sermons, working through issues with their siblings, controlling their emotions - the list goes on. Just remember*

though, they won't be perfect and get it right every time, but it definitely has helped them greatly.

Michelle, Mum to 4

From when I was a toddler, my parents were intentional about imparting the importance of developing Godly character. They spent many dedicated hours sharing the practical applications of traits like Attentiveness, Self-Control, Obedience, Gratefulness, Patience and many others through daily devotional and Bible reading times. We would look up Scripture passages related to the character quality, research illustrations from nature and form creative crafts such as table placemats that would remind us of the trait during the week.

Ultimately, the goal was not to turn us out as perfect little prince and princesses, but to facilitate growth in becoming like Jesus. Now, as a young adult, in a world where most people my age do not necessarily show obedience to authority, work hard, have gratitude and put others first, I can see how important this character training was at the beginning. Mum and Dad knew that I wouldn't just grow up and 'know' what was right – they had to teach and model it. For that I am so grateful.

Jerome, age 19

5

The Root Cause

What causes all the 'wet, sticky, smelly, brown patches' in the life of your toddler?

Basically, they are the result of a lack of self-control.

A toddler will naturally be self-centred, selfish, generally loud, unable to amuse themselves for any length of time, demanding, prone to outbursts of anger, picky with their food, uncooperative, destructive, unwilling to obey your instructions and unkind to others. They are like this because they do not have control over their words, emotions and actions.

You can sit back and accept this natural state or you can be proactive and positive and train your child to be self-controlled. A toddler can be others-focused, prone to sharing, generally quiet, able to amuse themselves for 20 – 40 minutes at a time, compliant, not prone to outbursts of anger, great eaters, co-operative, careful, willing to obey your instructions and kind to others.

Which toddler would you prefer?

The following suggestions in this book will not give you a perfect toddler, but they will help you train your child in self-control and give you a plan not only to avoid many of the sticky messes, but also to create a harmonious, happy environment. It will also enable you to greatly enjoy the toddler years with your child.

So, how do you teach a toddler to have self-control? You can train your child all day through their everyday activities of sleeping, eating, playing, visiting, shopping and so on. Mostly it is done through play. This approach is fun for the child and positive for you. By organising your daily activities into a flexible pattern, you will be providing the ideal environment for your child to progressively learn to control his or her words, actions and emotions.

The walls of a house provide the structure of a home and must be in place before you start to decorate the interior of the home. If you tried to start decorating before the plastering and painting was finished, you would be quite frustrated, wouldn't you? However, once the walls are finished you can make your home beautiful and enjoy watching the transformation. Likewise, your toddler will thrive in a flexible pattern for their day. Once that routine is in place, you will be able to effectively teach all the positive virtues that derive from having self-control.

Parenthood involves much more than simply keeping your child dressed, fed and amused. Each activity during your day is an opportunity to develop skills on a number of levels. You will be teaching your child physical, social and academic skills appropriate for their ages. Most importantly, however, you can use each activity to develop self-control in your toddler.

For example, as your toddler does a puzzle he will be developing his fine motor skills as he learns to place the puzzle piece in the right hole. As you talk about the pictures in your puzzle you will be increasing his academic knowledge. As he learns to sit and complete the puzzle he is learning to focus and concentrate, hence indirectly developing self-control.

Or, as your toddler plays outside she will be developing her gross motor skills. As she plays in her sandbox she will learn about pouring, measuring, digging and building. As you teach her to play outside for a continuous period she will learn self-play adeptness and self-control.

Or, when you feed your child you are doing more than simply meeting his nutritional needs. You can also be teaching him manners and conversational skills over the meal. You will also be indirectly teaching him self-control as he learns to wait quietly for the meal and then sit still to eat it. From your toddler's perspective, it is all fun play. From the parent's perspective, it is a valuable teaching experience.

I don't really get very excited about preparing sandwiches for lunch day after day. But I do get excited over seeing my toddler able to sit quietly for the whole meal and to watch the progress of his growing politeness and conversation skills. I don't particularly get excited over bathing my child every day. But I do get greatly excited over seeing my toddler develop the self-control to be able to sit and play quietly in the bath, and to remember the little rhymes or songs we sing during bath time every day.

Staying at home with my toddler is a privilege. It is also very challenging and has incredible rewards. Teaching your child to have self-control over his behaviours, attitudes and choices is one of the most precious gifts you can give him for life. It has great worth and is also eternally significant. Working on the cause of toddler messes is far more rewarding than simply reacting to them as they occur. Hence you will have a happy toddler and a happy mum too.

I have seen many families turned from chaos into order and calm within a few weeks simply by organising their day. You can do this too.

In the next few chapters I'll list the benefits of a daily pattern for parent and toddler. Then we'll look at the – what, why, when and how, of working out a weekly schedule that is right for you. Finally, I'll answer some of the questions I have received relating to this whole topic.

School Years

During the school years, the development of self-control is enhanced through daily chores. The control of self is needed to complete a task in a certain way at a certain time each day, even when they don't feel like doing it. Teaching one new chore each school holiday period will ensure you have a week or two of training and practice before the regular term begins.

Establishing a set time for homework will also enhance self-control during the school years. Completing the set activities, in the set way, at the same time each day requires control of the body, words and attitude. The work you put in here will stand you in good stead for the teen years.

It takes quite a lot of self-control to listen to the instructions of the soccer coach or to follow the steps of the ballet teacher. Having the commitment to turn up to practice and games or concerts at the expected time helps develop self-control. Encouraging your child to take responsibility for packing the required bits into their bag in a timely manner for each session and unpacking on their return is also consolidating the self-control to take ownership of their possessions.

Your biggest task in this season regarding self-control is to teach the appropriate expression of emotions. You are not suppressing any emotion. Your child can feel incredibly excited, angry, sad, disappointed, frustrated, scared and bored. It is the appropriate expression of these emotions that will aid emotional self-control. One child would scream at an extremely high-pitched tone when pleased with a surprise. They needed to learn to express this pleasure in a manner that did not hurt the ears of those around them. A child who was feeling grumpy or angry could feel that way in the privacy of their own room. Please note, it is not effective to try to talk with a child about his emotional outburst in the middle of the outburst. Have them wait in their room until they are calm and ready to talk it through calmly. Sometimes, it is even best to have this chat the next morning.

Teen Years

Most of the teens at school make decisions, or react in the moment, according to their emotions. Their feelings scream at them to be obeyed. They are powerful and strong. They do what feels good or acceptable in that moment. They rarely pre-plan their responses. They don't complete their assessment tasks because they felt like watching a movie. They have a drink at the party because everyone else is, and they purchase that new shirt because it looks good there on the rack, regardless of whether they can afford it or if they need it. These teens are characterised by being moody and disagreeable. They are ungrateful and have a sense of entitlement. They do not feel right because they are not doing right.

These situations all require self-control. The self-control of emotions to complete school tasks before watching a movie, the self-control of actions to not do something in a group, even if everyone else is doing it, and the self-control of thoughts to not purchase an item without first considering the necessity of that item.

There are some wonderful teens at school who are characterised by self-control. They set a schedule and complete all assessments on time. They stand firm in group situations and defend the one who is being picked on. They make their own choices regarding acceptable behaviours. They budget their money and make wise purchases, often favouring the Op shops or even making their own clothes over new clothes. These teens have a happy countenance, and are engaging and fun. They feel right because they are doing right.

So be encouraged, the work you have invested in self-control training will reap much fruit in the teen years. Having the responsibility of a part-time job, the expectation of regular household responsibilities, and the deadlines for school assessments provide natural opportunities for continuing to develop self-control.

Proverbs 16:32 'Better a patient person than a warrior, one with self-control than one who takes a city.'

> My children's ages span 3 – 19 years, that's a lot of years I have known Mel's philosophy on Toddlers! Seven children, seven lots of Toddler years and I can honestly say they have been Terrific. Using a flexible schedule and having it written up with pictures, has meant my little ones run to see what they should be doing. It gives them security, helps me plan, and helps me have time to get things done, it brings peace in our home and when things do go pear shaped, I can see why – usually we're off schedule!
>
> Training in character is a high priority for the early years and recently rereading Mel's books, I was, again, so grateful for her practical, simple wisdom. Using Terrific Toddlers in teaching and training our children has helped me be intentional and proactive in planning activities and developing character. This has made our Toddler Years such a blessing.
>
> **Kathryn B, Mum to 7**

I could write all day about the things I've learned on my parenting journey (often through my own mistakes) but most of them are simply the result of training in one particular virtue - self-control. Now that my 3 children have grown into young adults (19, 19, and 18), I am reaping the benefits of years of hard work. I have always loved them and treasured my time with them, but the last few years are when I've actually been able to just relax and enjoy them.

They have always been given leadership roles beyond their years, people would ask to 'borrow' them for weekends even when they didn't have kids of their own. I believe this was because they were taught to obey the first time an instruction was given, and they were successfully learning self-control. Now they are all very successful in their workplaces because they know how to respect authority, hold their tongues, control their 'tone' of voice, show initiative, give their best and lead by example.

They've never been afraid to be different, and are confident in who they are. I'm so very thankful for the wise women like Mel whose advice gave me the confidence to parent with a purpose and standard that went against the norm. It was hard but rewarding, and was sometimes lonely as I was judged for setting and keeping firm boundaries. Now though - I am bursting with happiness as I watch my 3 shining lights take on the world and reap the benefits of the lessons we learned together along the way.

Rochelle, Mum to 3

A quick thought is that the benefits of toddler training are not just for the children. Many a time my own personality has benefitted from learning more about self-control, what words come out of my mouth and other development areas. They are always watching us and therefore we must truly practice what we preach.

Also, the importance of our end goal of friendship must be remembered as we struggle through the training. Where are we headed? It makes the journey which can be rough and challenging truly worthwhile.

Kylie, Mum to 3

Looking back on my years as a child/teen, I have come to realise that I am grateful for a lot of values that my parents instilled in me during that time. One of the first values that comes to mind is respect. The reason why, I believe, is because I use respect every day. When I respect someone, I am acknowledging the person as a human being, with their own rights, talents, and property. Respect helps me to put others before myself, and keeps me from being self-centred, as respect requires that I treat others how I prefer to be treated. It also assists me with practical life situations, such as giving an elderly person my seat, or being careful with borrowed property. Respect is a universal language, and something we all use. I am very grateful that my parents saw the value in respect, and strove to impart it to me through their parenting.

Megan, age 19

6

Benefits for Parents

Having a flexible pattern for the week is so very good for both parents, especially the main caregiver. Here are some of the benefits parents most enjoy from having a plan for their week. Do you want to have these benefits too? Can you add some more?

Toddler Years

- An hour, or more, to yourself each day
- A tidy house all through the day
- Don't have lots of toys to clean up each evening after the child has gone to bed
- Have a toddler who regularly and happily picks up her own toys
- Balance between completing chores and playing with the child is obtained each day
- Have very few instances of 'No' in your day
- Be able to clean and cook without chaos reigning in the house
- Have time to be out with friends and still meet the responsibilities of home
- Have evenings free to spend time with spouse or friends as all tasks are completed during the day
- Feel calm and in control – most days!
- Have a toddler who helps with the chores (great start for the future)
- More adequately manage the usually horrible late afternoon hours
- Have uninterrupted conversations on the phone and while visiting friends

- Have your own emotional, spiritual, social, intellectual and physical needs met over the course of the week
- Spend positive time with each child every day
- Feel fulfilled at the end of each week - not frustrated
- Don't have a toddler nagging you to play or read when you are trying to get chores done, as there is a time for everything
- Have far fewer outbursts (times when you lose it) because all tasks are done in an orderly manner – most of the time
- A calm and orderly household for your partner to arrive home to
- Be proud of your toddler and happy to be out and about with him

School Years

- Regular time for homework means less nagging
- Regular time for music practice means less nagging
- Regular time for chores means less nagging
- Regular playdate time (e.g. only on Friday afternoon) means less nagging
- One-to-one time is enjoyed each week
- Regular sleep patterns ensure less tiredness issues

Teen Years

- Household responsibilities well-established so completed regularly and without fuss
- Pattern of weekend sleep-in is appreciated
- Enjoy mostly positive interactions
- Family night is simply part of regular week so no negotiation is needed
- Family courtesies such as cleaning up after yourself and curfews are clearly established, and so are not regularly debated
- Enjoy one-on-one time each week

We now have four young adults in our family and it is clear to see the difference that the training we did in the early years is affecting their character now. When our children were little, they had relatively little issues to deal with - learning how to sit in a trolley while I did the shopping or learning to share with their friends and siblings were all pretty small, though important, lessons to learn.

We've found that as our children have grown bigger, so too have the issues they are facing and also the consequences of their behaviour. If you don't have the self-control to sit still in the trolley, you might hurt yourself, or at least, make life a bit more difficult for Mum while she shops.

However, if you don't have the self-control to focus on the road when you are behind the wheel of a car, the consequences can be dire. Terrific Toddlers helped us to lay an invaluable foundation in the hearts of our children and we are incredibly grateful to Mel for putting together such a protocol and helpful resource.

Charissa, Mum to 4

On the first night of our cruise, as we entered the dining room with our two-year-old, you could sense the dismay of others. They were expecting to have their fine dining interrupted by the typical two-year-old tantrums. Instead, they were treated to a little boy who sat quietly and ate the food he was given. A little boy who then played quietly in his high chair with the few toys there. By the end of the cruise, he had won over the whole dining room with his good behaviour and his gorgeous smile.

Kathryn M, Mum to 2

7

Benefits for your Child

Having a flexible pattern for your week is so very good for your child. Here are a few of the main benefits that many children enjoy as a result of a planned week. Would you like your child to have these benefits too? Can you add some more?

Toddler Years

- Is generally happy and content
- Hears 'No' very few times in his day
- Is predominantly praised each day (which is great for emotional well-being)
- Enjoys a balance of play activities each day – quiet and noisy, indoor and outdoor
- Enjoys the security of an orderly and calm environment
- Is free to be a child and simply play - not make unnecessary decisions all day
- Learns to concentrate for sustained periods of time and hence can greatly enjoy each toy fully
- Experiences true creativity and imaginative play
- Accepts and appreciates (over time) that mum and dad are in charge
- Does not need to constantly ask for things as he knows there is time for each activity
- Enjoys a balance between time just with mum, time just with dad, time to play alone and family time

- Feels esteemed as he practices tidiness and personal responsibility each day
- Learns to be a valuable and needed member of the family by contributing to chores
- Has her emotional, spiritual, intellectual, social and physical needs met each week
- Feels good because he is learning to do good
- Has a self-disciplined and productive lifestyle modelled to her every day
- Learns that other people are important too
- Experiences the joy that comes from reading
- Enjoys a wide variety of experiences at an early age due to his good behaviour, as mum and dad are happy to take him out
- Is enjoyed by others

School Years
- Regular time for homework means less protesting and complaining
- Regular time for music practice means less protesting and complaining
- Regular time for chores means less protesting and complaining
- Regular playdate time (e.g. only on Friday afternoon) means less asking during the week
- Regular sleep patterns ensure less tiredness issues
- Child feels like a valuable member of the family unit due to their regular contributions via chores and family night participation
- Enjoys the balance of school, free play, family time and their hobby
- Achieves their best at school due to completing all tasks
- Performs their best in their chosen hobby as they listen to and follow instructions
- Enjoys positive time with siblings each week
- Enjoys mostly positive interactions with parents
- Enjoys special one-on-one time with parent each week

Teen Years

- Household responsibilities well-established so completed regularly and without fuss
- Pattern of weekend sleep-in is appreciated
- Enjoy mostly positive interactions
- Family night is simply part of regular week so no negotiation is needed
- Family courtesies such as cleaning up after yourself and curfews are clearly established so are not regularly debated
- Enjoys one-on-one time with siblings each week
- Have the best chance of pursuing their chosen career as they are performing their best at school
- Have the opportunity to excel at a high level in their chosen hobby as they practice and dedicate themselves to excellence
- Enjoys mostly positive interactions with parents
- Able to balance responsibilities of school, part-time work, hobby and community or church involvement
- Enjoys special one-on-one time with parent each week

With the foundation of Terrific Toddlers and character training in their life, our teens, and pre-teens, now draw up their own schedules so they can plan and use their time efficiently. They use these plans to guide their Bible study, school work, family time, sport and free time during the week. It is a blessing to see them using their time wisely.

Darren, Dad to 7

8

Balancing Acts

As you begin to plan your week, you must keep in mind the needs of each member of your family. Your flexible weekly pattern should enable you to meet the emotional, spiritual, social, intellectual and physical needs of each person.

Emotional – special times for two people to spend together to esteem, praise and encourage each other. This could be husband and wife, parent and child, or child and child. Also, time playing alone encourages imagination, appreciation of solitude and creativity.

Spiritual – a quiet time each day for renewing and refreshing the soul and focusing on the eternal value of life. Also, time spent teaching the child your spiritual values and holy teachings.

Social – a number of occasions each week for individuals to interact with those outside the family. 'Mums' need a chance to interact as 'ladies' as frequently as possible (i.e. to spend time outside their role as parent). Toddlers love to be out and experiencing different situations.

Intellectual – Mums need to keep learning and reading either formally or informally and have other interests outside parenting. Toddlers need to be taught their numbers, letters, colours, shapes, animals, seasons and so on.

Physical – Time needs to be set aside every day for toddlers to run and play in an active way, some will need an hour while others need three hours to burn up their boundless energy! Mums and dads also need time for exercise each week for their own health.

Wouldn't you love to have all of this in your week? I know I feel happier and healthier when I have a balanced week. Do you feel frustrated at times with the conflict of trying to;
- Constantly keep the house clean and tidy?
- Cope with the daily piles of washing?
- Creatively plan and prepare meals?

and
- Spend quality time with your child in play?
- Provide appropriate learning opportunities?
- Simply have fun with your child?

and
- Enjoy time out for yourself?
- Pursue a relaxing hobby or craft?
- Keep in touch with your friends and family?

Some amazing women can do all of this naturally, every week. However, most of us need to plan it out. A flexible pattern will enable you to balance all these things. Isn't that great?

It will take you between three days and three weeks to establish a flexible pattern into your family. It will be hard work during that initial phase. However, after that you will reap many rewards for all the years to come. The early effort is repaid many, many, many times over. So, do persevere. Every family will have a different routine, depending on the number and ages of children in the family, and the unique needs of each member.

One of my favourite quotes is this:

'If you keep on doing what you have been doing, you will keep on getting what you have been getting.'

If you are enjoying being with your toddler each day and if you are personally enjoying a balance of activities and friendships, then you will probably continue doing what you are doing. However, if you are not enjoying being with your toddler each day, and if you are frustrated by the lack of time for activities and friendships for yourself, then maybe it's time to think about whether to keep doing what you have been doing.

It makes sense to try something else, and therefore achieve a different result.

Convinced? Let's get to it.

School Years

Establishing a weekly pattern that meets the physical, emotional, spiritual, social and intellectual needs of your school aged child will take some thought and planning. Do resist the urge to over-fill their week with organised activities. Having most afternoons just to play freely in the backyard will give them time to create, problem-solve, think, explore, dream, imagine, experiment, get muddy and dirty and sweaty, and to simply have fun. Get them being active each weekend with their set sport or family bushwalks, beach visits, park plays, bike-riding and a long outside play time.

Find a church that has an active kids program and establish good morals and ethics in the heart of your child. Plan a balance of family activities with other families and playdates with friends. Allow time and provide resources for them to pursue their interest in planes, cars, horses, animals or whatever. Your thoughtful weekly pattern will aid the development of a well-rounded child and will be establishing life-long habits.

Teen Years

As I observe the teens that I teach each week, balance is not a word that characterises them. They tend to be focused on one main thing. For some the focus is sport, for others it is music, or drama, or cars, or fashion, or their studies. For many, the focus is on their friends and having fun experiences and seeing the latest movie and buying the newest gadget.

If you have had a flexible pattern for your week from the toddler years, then you are much more able to influence your teen to have a week that provides a balance of social, emotional, intellectual, spiritual and physical elements. If this is a new idea for you, it is still possible to encourage these things. Sitting down with your teen at a café at the start of a new school year can be a good starting point. Look at what they need to have in their week (e.g. school hours, soccer practice, violin lesson) and then timetable each event in. Talk through the best time for chores, social activities and relaxation time.

When you have your weekly one-to-one afternoon tea, you can quickly review how the pattern for the week is going and what areas need to be adjusted. They may or may not really follow it, but addressing the issue regularly will keep them thinking about balance. Balance is crucial for the mental well-being of your teen so it is important to gently and persistently work on this.

Hebrews 12:1 'Let us run with perseverance the race marked out for us.'

> *Using everyday activities as training opportunities to instil positive virtues lends meaning to the cyclical nature of most women's lives. This is immensely encouraging and will enable mothers to train their toddlers not just to be good, but to be the best that they can be.*
>
> **Jo, Mum to 4**

> *Jess (aged 20) and I had a chuckle over the phone last night about how annoying one of her customers had been. They had spoken unkindly when they could easily have been polite.*
>
> *That lady's mum obviously hadn't taught her about using a kind tone of voice! Tone of voice, again, is not an easy thing to teach to a primary school aged child.*
>
> *It takes a lot of repetition of instructions.*
>
> *It takes patience to stay calm when you need to insist that your kids need to apologise for not speaking in a kind tone.*
>
> *But when you realise that in the end, you will have an adult child who is a blessing to everyone she meets (shopkeepers, kids she*

babysits, the older customers at work, her boss), you realise the hard work was worth it!

Galatians 6:9. Memorise it! Say it to yourself as you wait for the kids to calm down enough to talk to. It's worth it!

Al, Mum to 2

9

Flexibility

As you read through the following chapters, please keep in mind the importance of being flexible. This simply means being willing to adjust to the personalities and circumstances of your day. Your plan is meant to be a guide for your day, not the law. The activities I have listed in the next chapter are simply suggestions. You may have a much simpler plan for your day, or it may be much tighter. Your day will suit you and your family.

Please note that you will have plenty of spontaneous moments with your child during each day. You are not marching through each activity in a regimented fashion. There is always time for hugs and kisses, and to listen to the new discoveries or stories your child loves to share with you. You will share the daily sorrows and delights of your child's life within your basic plan for the day.

You may only be home three days a week, or you may be home five days a week. That will depend on your own social needs, the number of children you have and the stage your family is at. The best place to train your child is in your own home. If you are out all day every day then you will be missing out on the best opportunities to train your child. However, staying home all day every day is not healthy for you, or your toddler. Find a sensible balance in the middle that works for you. Most mums I speak to aim to be home for three or four days each week.

My day did not always turn out like the day written out on the notice board in the kitchen. I often needed to be flexible.

As the parent, you will determine the length of each activity. You may initially expect an activity to last for 10 to 15 minutes. Over the next few months you will slowly extend that time to 30 or 40 minutes for each activity. However, you will have days when you need to be flexible. You may extend the length of an activity if the child is struggling with it on a particular day.

If the child or yourself is ill, then you may both spend the entire day in front of the television or sitting on the lounge with a few books. On a gorgeous sunny day, you may choose to have most of your activities outside. On a very wet and cold day you will be doing most of your activities inside.

Phone calls and visitors are not interruptions to your day; they are a part of it. Graciously answer the phone or invite your caller in. Adjust your day to make them feel welcome.

If your toddler is uncharacteristically quite tired and grumpy, then simply give him an early nap or put him to bed earlier for the night. Sam's bedtime was usually 6:30 pm but there were many nights when he was grumpy and so was in bed by 6:00 pm. Be flexible.

Also, be flexible over your whole week. You may usually be home three to five days each week and out for shopping, errands, visiting or child-based activities for two to four days each week. If, however, you are working on a new behaviour then you may stay home a little more for a week or two. There may also be times when you need to be out every day for a week or two. That is all okay. Be flexible. Most weeks will be a balance of at home days and out days.

Flexibility is important as you respond to the different personalities of each of your children. One child may need far more physical activity than another child. One may need extra times of quiet away from the busyness of the house. If one has a particular interest, then attempt to work that in too. One child may love books and another music, so do include extra time for those interests in your plan.

Every family is unique and you will pursue a plan that is best for your family. Think through the principles behind each part of the plan and decide if they will be helpful for you and your child. If you discover other activities that progressively build self-control into your child's life in a fun and proactive way, please do share them with me. I would love to hear from you (my email address is on the back page).

School Years

Flexibility will also be needed throughout the school years. At times, I would keep my fragile child home from school to simply spend time with them and fill up their emotional tank. Other times, I may keep the child who is struggling with an issue at school home for a day, just to give them a day of relief and some extra tender loving care. Other times, it was the child that was developing an attitude or a habit that I was not happy with that would stay home so I could ask some questions to try and discover the heart issue behind the behaviour. Very rarely, after a particularly full time of visitors, I would keep all three at home to simply have a day of games and fun to help us reconnect as a family.

The other key time for flexibility is during the school holidays. We had a more relaxed pattern for these days and a rough plan for a day out (often with friends) followed by a day at home. Each home day itself included outside play each morning, an hour of quiet independent play each afternoon, hobby or interest time after that for a couple of hours, and then chores, dinner and family time. It was simple yet balanced and worked well for all the school years.

Teen Years

Flexibility in the teen years will be needed in relation to school activities. School exams, camp week, sport events, carnivals and musical productions will require adjustments to the weekly pattern. Other outside influences will include sports finals season, dance competitions and concerts, musical rehearsals, part-time work rosters, church meetings and learning to drive.

The expectation for attendance at family events such as Birthdays and Christmas, sibling sports finals or dance concerts was clearly established well before each event so adjustments could be made to the part-time work roster or other regular commitment.

It is also important to show that as the parent you can be reasonable and flexible as needed. We live an hour out from the city so if a teen was attending a concert or event there, then the curfew for that night would be extended. If the 18th birthday party of a close friend clashed with a minor family event, then the teen would be given the freedom to choose between the two. Remember that the weekly plan is there to help, not rule.

Ecclesiastes 3:1 'There is a time for everything, and a season for every activity under the heavens.'

10

Daily Activities – One

Well, now let's look at the specific activities to put into your flexible pattern.

I'll work through a sample day here and give you an idea of what a day at home with your toddler may look like. As we go through, I'll explain some of the reasons behind each activity and the benefits for mum, dad and toddler. I'll then add a quick comment for the school and teen years for each activity.

Morning Start

Toddler Years

It is very important that you, as the parent, are in charge right from the very beginning of the day. It sets the tone for the rest of the day. Start your day at the time you choose.

Your toddler will probably gain a sibling or two over the next few years. Think ahead. If all your children learn to rise at the same time each day then you don't have the early birds depriving your sleepy ones of their needed rest. That will help eliminate starting your day with a cranky toddler who really needed an extra hour of sleep. Another benefit is that you will not rise to find that your toddler has been into the cupboards or bathroom, to make a huge mess to start off your day.

Since I am a night owl myself, it is so wonderful to know that my child will not be rising before 7:00 am every day. If I were woken at 5:00 am or 6:00 am each day, I would be a very grumpy mummy – not a good start to the day for my child or myself!

Your toddler will be practicing self-control and patience as he learns to wait quietly in bed until his favourite song comes on. He is also learning to think of others – to be quiet so that everyone else can get the sleep they need. Isn't that great? To think your little one can be learning all those things before your day has even started.

It will take a little effort to enforce this in your home, but it will be well worth the early work. Use an alarm clock or favourite song to signal when the child is allowed out of bed. Be very clear with your expectations. I expected my children to stay in bed and to be quiet before the alarm went off. There was to be no talking, to themselves or to each other. They were permitted to read, if they woke a little early. If you have a very early riser (i.e. one who wakes up with the birds!) you may want to place a few books on the end of the bed for her to read until it is time to get out of bed.

If your child is currently waking, and getting out of bed, at 5:30 am and you want your day to start at 7:00 am, then it will take a few weeks to get there. Set your alarm for 6:00 am for a week, then 6:30 am for the next week and so on, until you get to 7:00 am. Sounds impossible? It will work if you have appropriate rewards for compliance and a suitable consequence for non-compliance. More on that later.

Note: I often moved the alarm to 8:00 am on the weekends – so we could all have a sleep in. Little ones hardly ever noticed the difference!

School Years

Keep a set time for the start of each school day. This will ensure there is enough time to get ready each morning without the last-minute fluster. If you find that your child is struggling to wake on Monday morning after a later morning start on Saturday and Sunday, then adjust back to their usual time, or keep it within 30 minutes of their usual wake-up time so that Monday morning is not a huge adjustment.

Teen Years

Most parents of teens agree that their teens struggle to get up in the morning! This is often because they are not disciplined about going to bed at a reasonable time. With your young teens, insist on a set wake-up time. This will ensure they are able to be at school on time each day. For your older teen, you can encourage them to set a regular start time to their day but ultimately it is their choice.

Breakfast

Toddler Years

Before coming to the table, I expected each child to make their own beds. I did this right from the first day they are moved out of their cot to their big bed and they loved to feel important. At first, they simply pull up their blankets, but by the time they are five years old, they should be able to do it fairly well. Gradually raise your standard and improvement will be evident. Keep it positive, praise their effort and ignore the lumps!

Have each child sit on the same chair each day at the table – you don't need to have an argument about who sits where, first thing in the morning. Just clearly and calmly state who is sitting where. Remember your kitchen is not a restaurant – do not take orders.

You choose the cereal, and also the:

- topping for the cereal
- small spoon or the big spoon
- spread for the toast
- way the toast is cut
- type of drink
- temperature of the drink (cold or warm)
- order in which the meal will be eaten
- type of cup
- type of plate

In other words . . . Everything!

Why is this so important? As the parent, you don't mind if the toast is cut into squares or rectangles, do you? As the parent, you don't mind if they have vegemite or peanut butter, do you? Why? These are very benign issues to us as adults. From our adult perspective, it doesn't really matter how the toast is cut. From our adult perspective, it doesn't really matter if the spread is vegemite or peanut butter.

The important point here is **who** chooses if the toast is cut into squares or rectangles. Who chooses if the spread is peanut butter or vegemite. If the child is making this choice, and hundreds and hundreds of other small insignificant choices all day, every day, then he begins to feel as if he is in charge. So, he will question your authority in a huge and horrible way at other times during the day (those messes on your white carpet).

I have found that as I made all the (seemingly) little decisions in my toddler's day, then I had very, very few big messes to deal with during those toddler years. Think it through yourself. Does it make sense to you? Can you see how, from your toddler's perspective, he will feel like he is the boss if he is making decisions all day?

Of course, occasionally he gets to choose his favourite ice cream or a special video. From the age of three, you will also start to give him limited options (e.g. painting or drawing now?) so that he can learn how to make decisions for himself. By the time he is six or seven years of age you will find that he can make many good decisions for himself because you have firstly modelled appropriate decision-making skills to him, and then gradually allowed him to make more and more of his own decisions.

Note: If you calmly decide to take away your toddler's choices, you will have an 'explosion' for three to five days, as they react to the change. After that, your days will be much calmer, and your toddler will be happier too.

At the end of breakfast, you may leave your younger child in the highchair while you do the dishes and clean the kitchen. A child can sit and watch or have one small book to read. You won't have a messy kitchen to clean up afterwards and won't have to try and get back to it later in the day. Most importantly though, your toddler is learning patience, slowly becoming aware that mum has work to do and is not just there to play with all day: he is building a little more self-control.

Or you may have your older toddler help you clean up. I started by having my little one carry her plastic plate or cup to the sink. Later you can teach her to wipe the table, wipe up some of the (unbreakable) dishes or sweep the floor. Don't underestimate what she can do. If you start small, do it every morning, give her lots of praise and keep it fun, you can have a four-year-old who can tidy the kitchen for you.

At the end of breakfast time we would read the Bible and revise any Scripture verses we had learned. As soon as my children could talk I would have them learn parts of the Bible and read it every day. By starting early, I hoped it would simply become part of every day for their lifetime. This time was very short, often only a few minutes, and we had the Bible close to the table and the verses written out and pinned up in the kitchen so it was very easy to transition into this time.

School Years

You can have limited choices for weekday breakfast. For example, my children could choose between Weetbix or Cornflakes for their cereal, and two or three spreads for their toast. They are most capable of making this themselves and popping their dishes in the dishwasher and wiping down their placemat. Also, teach them to do one extra chore at this time such as sweep the floor, wipe down the cupboard, empty the bin or spray the sink.

Teen Years

Give your teen the responsibility of cooking breakfast for the family on Saturday or Sunday. They can experiment with bacon and eggs, French toast, breakfast rolls, pancakes and so on. This ensures you have breakfast together as a family and gives them an opportunity to serve their family. Do ensure they clean up afterwards too. This greatly encouraged my use-every-pot-in-the-kitchen child to consider cleaning up their dishes as they go.

Room Play

Toddler Years

This is one of the best parts of the day for a toddler, and for mum. The child learns to play quietly for a whole hour by herself, in her own room.

The toddler is learning to play for a good length of time with just a few toys, and she is also learning to be creative and use her imagination with her toys. The child also learns to play in an orderly manner with her toys as she returns one toy to the shelf before playing with the next. Your toddler is also learning self-control as she stays in her room to play and doesn't keep wandering out. Most importantly, she comes to realise that mum has other things to do in her day, other than just play with her.

Mum can have a whole hour to have a shower, relax for a few minutes, put the washing out, mop the kitchen floor and get organised for the day. Each child has the peace and the space to play without being interrupted by their siblings, and you don't have any conflicts to deal with first thing in the morning. This time is great if you have one child – simply wonderful if you have two or more! Some mothers use room play just before dinner, so the children are quiet, not playing (or fighting) with their siblings and dinner can be prepared without interruptions.

Are you thinking, 'My active two-year-old could never learn to do this?' Be encouraged, she can! You will need to begin with a very small amount of time – maybe only 10 minutes for the first week. Clearly explain to her what you expect – for her to play in this room, with these toys. You choose the few toys for her. If you can have the toys that are just for room play, this will greatly help you succeed here. Change the toys every few weeks to keep your child interested.

You will need to hover, just out of sight for the first week, to ensure your child is safe and is not playing with other toys, drawers and so on. You will not get any time yourself for the first few days, but if you are calm and consistent, you will soon have an hour to yourself for years to come.

It is helpful to have something that clearly defines when this time ends, either a buzzing timer or the end of a special music or story recording that the child enjoys. Give your child an abundance of praise for playing quietly and appropriately during this time. As your child happily plays for 10 minutes for a week, then you can gradually increase this room time over the next few weeks.

Have her pack up the toys with you. Do it in an orderly fashion, packing up the books first, and then packing up the trucks. This is showing her how to pack up and the importance of taking responsibility for her own clean up, eventually! It also means you don't have an untidy room to come back to later.

If you need to do the final straightening of the room, have her sit on the bed to watch you, she will only be sitting for a brief moment, and she is practicing a little patience and not getting out of sight and into mischief. If your child comes out of the room or tries to chat to you during this time, you need to have a calm and consistent consequence to motivate her to comply with you. More on that later.

Most mums love this idea and are very keen to have it occurring in their own home each day. Please note, if you try to implement this into a day that has no order and structure in the rest of the day, then it will not be successful.

The self-control that you are teaching and modelling in your entire day is what is needed for each activity to be successful in your day. Also note that if your toddler is making lots of little decisions all day, then they will not be willing to obey you and stay in their room.

What if your child just sits in the room and won't play? That's fine, just keep working on increasing the room play time up to an hour and praise her for staying in her room during that time. She will eventually play.

If you do want to encourage her to play, then set a task for her to do at the beginning of room time, e.g. 'Do this puzzle' or 'Build a tower from these blocks', just to get her started.

School Years

Do continue with room time throughout the school years. A half an hour of independent play time each afternoon gives each child the chance to pursue their hobby or interest uninterrupted. In the school holidays, extend this time to two hours and let them develop the ability to be on their own and to increase their task persistence skills.

Teen Years

With technology, teens can now be constantly connected to each other and the world. If you establish an hour of technology-free time each week day you are helping your teen have invaluable time to think, dream, plan, imagine, create and problem-solve. This time of rest is a great chance to read, pursue their hobby or interest and develop new skills.

Focus Play

Toddler Years

This was my most favourite time of the entire day. This was when I focused solely on my toddler. It was a fun time and one characterised by lots of cuddles and affirmative words. The main aim was to build up my relationship with my child and fill up his little emotional tank so that he feels totally loved.

Some days we sat for 10 minutes, other days it was closer to 50 minutes. We would read, play imaginative games, learn some academics, bake cookies or cakes, do craft projects together, work on puzzles together, colour-in, and so on. The child loves this time and looks forward to it each day. I have always had focus play in the morning and I find that my toddler is then quite happy to play by himself for extended periods of time for the rest of the day.

By planning to have this special time early in the day, I could then move through my cleaning and cooking without feeling guilty that I'm not playing with my child, or feeling frustrated by the constant interruptions from a toddler who just wants a little attention. Hence mum and toddler are both happy.

Through the play activities during this time, I focus on positively teaching my child some attitudes or behaviours that we are currently working on. I will choose one thing to briefly teach each day. For example, if you have noticed that your child is struggling to share his toys with his friends you may act out a little puppet show with your child that talks about why we share or how we share. Or you could find or draw some pictures showing some children sharing their toys nicely.

If you are working on teaching your child basic manners you could have a little tea party and practice your 'Please' and 'Thank you'' as you enjoy your water and sugar cups of tea. Or the dolls could act out being polite to each other as they play. If you are working on helping your child not to whine you could have his trucks use a whiny voice and then a nice voice as they talk to each other. Positively talk about why we don't whine. Or you could have a number of small cookies and practice having a toy bear ask, in a nice voice, for a cookie (and getting one) and then asking in a whining voice (and not getting one). The possibilities are endless.

Be creative and have fun with your child. Keep the teaching part to just a few minutes and ensure your tone is positive and encouraging. By training in this happy time, you greatly minimise the number of 'messes' you have in the rest of your day and you also greatly reduce the size of them too. Rather than simply reacting when a 'mess' appears, you can be proactively working to ensure they don't appear, or are very small if they do.

Always have your child help you pack up at the end of each activity so that your house is staying in order and you don't have to go back and tidy up later in your day. Your child can sit still just for a minute or two until you are ready to go on to the next activity in their day. Each of these little moments of waiting during your day are helping your child build up his self-control and will greatly help his sustained attention skills at other times in your day.

Do you have more than one child? It is vitally important that each child has this focus play each day and it is possible to plan your day so they each have 10 – 20 minutes alone with mum. It involves some careful planning, and a little trial and error at first, but you can find a plan that works for your family. You may have one child watching a video, playing outside or drawing while you have focus time with another. I know families with four and five children who even manage to do this.

School Years

During the school years, the daily focus time will revolve around their current interest. So sometimes we would colour-in together, play board games, do a jigsaw puzzle, build a LEGO village, or dress up the dolls. Weekly focus time was usually just a milkshake or an ice-cream. Often these little trips out did not reap any significant conversations (my boys, in particular, were often more interested in the cars that were passing by the window than in talking) but it was setting up the pattern of showing them that they were important to me.

Teen Years

During the teen years, the regular focus time with my boys involved one-on-one basketball games in the backyard, or table tennis matches. It also involved late night chats. This was tricky at times, as I would often be ready for sleep, but being available during this time proved invaluable as it was when they would often share their heart. Occasionally we would watch a major sporting event together or have a meal out.

Outside Play

Toddler Years

All children need to run and play in the fresh air each day to get exercise and to learn gross motor skills. If you spend a little time ensuring your yard is safe, then children will be able to play outside by themselves for up to an hour each day. Obviously, you will listen and watch every few minutes to ensure their safety.

It takes a lot of self-control to play outside for the length of time that mum or dad has determined. Your child is also learning to be busy and active independently, and gradually understands that mum and dad have other things to do in their day for themselves and for other members of the family too. During this time, I completed my household chores for the morning, caught up on correspondence, emails and phone calls or, on my lazy days, I read a book or the newspaper.

Your toddler will naturally want to come in and out during this time, but with a little encouragement she will come to love playing outside for a solid block of time. Another advantage of this is that you will not have sand, dirt or water tramped onto your floors all day, or flies and mosquitoes getting in through a constantly opening door.

Initially, you may encourage your child to be outside by herself for 10 – 20 minutes. You can start her off on an activity (for example, digging for a few minutes in the sand) or maybe provide a morning snack at the start of this time. When she is happily playing for this length of time then you can gradually increase it over the next few weeks.

Bikes, balls, climbing equipment and a sandbox are all ideal for this age group. For variety, we would sometimes fill up small containers with water, blow bubbles, paint the fence with water, run through a sprinkler, use outdoor chalk on the paths, do nature craft activities, provide a large cardboard box (or boxes) for imaginative play or go for a walk around the nearby streets discovering 'treasures' or jumping in the rain puddles.

Toward the end of outside play I would often play with my toddler by catching, kicking, bouncing or rolling a ball, by playing cricket or T-ball, roller skating (on the pre-school skates that barely roll), building roads or mountains in the sand, explore the garden and so on, then we pack up together for all the reasons previously mentioned.

If you have a very active child then it is very important that he or she learns how to run and play outside for at least an hour each day. The child who has boundless energy needs a positive outlet for this or you may experience problems later in the day, particularly in the late afternoon. My Sam was extremely active and so he had at least two (very long) outside play periods each day.

School Years

Do choose a sport for your child to be regularly involved in for the school years. You may need to try a few until you find what they most enjoy. Let them try one sport for a year, and give them the opportunity of choosing a different sport for the next year. This teaches them to commit to one thing for a season, but still affords them the chance to try a few different things. Plan active pursuits on the weekends and for family holidays. During these years, you are establishing important life-long habits for physical health that will benefit every area of their life.

Teen Years

Every year it seems that fewer and fewer of the teens I interact with are regularly participating in physical activity. This is even more true for the girls. Do model an active lifestyle yourself. Continue to encourage your teen to have a regular physical activity each week, even during their senior years of schooling. Allow them the freedom to try a new sport such as circus tricks, gym classes, cross-fit training, boxing, mountain-biking, stand-up paddle boarding or trail running. Try and do something physical together with them. My daughter and I set a goal and trained to run a half-marathon together - which I won by half a step!

11

Daily Activities – Two

I hope you are beginning to appreciate all the benefits that derive from implementing a positive plan into each day. Mum and toddler and child and teen are happy. I found it so exciting to be able to enjoy a productive and varied day with my toddler that was also fun. Let's now look at what you may include in the rest of your day.

Lunch

Toddler Years

Lunch is much more than a time to meet your toddler's nutritional needs. It can also be a time to train your child in self-control. You can give your child a sandwich to eat as he wanders around the house. However, not only will you have crumbs and bits of food to clean up later, you have also missed an opportunity to train.

Have your child sit quietly at the table while you prepare lunch. Use a highchair or a booster seat with a strap until he has enough self-control to sit on a big chair independently. It only takes a couple of minutes to make a sandwich and cut up some fruit. Again, you make the decisions concerning every part of the meal. As you work you can go through the alphabet or nursery rhymes together. Give your child lots of praise for sitting quietly and patiently.

I focus on teaching table manners over lunch. It is the meal where I am best able to focus on this. Be patient and teach one rule of etiquette at a time. There are many table rules that your child needs to learn but you have plenty of time to teach each one. Be creative and have fun as you teach your child the how and why of table manners.

School Years

During the school years, establish the pattern of eating real food for lunch during the week. Over the weekend, have them make their own and clean up their own, or to help a family member prepare this meal for the rest of the family. If you start this when they are five years old, then by the time they are 12 years of age they will be able to do this independently.

Teen Years

During the teen years, continue to encourage your teen to eat real food for their weekday lunch. Many teens choose to skip lunch at school and this has a noticeable effect on their ability to concentrate in their afternoon lessons. So, do ensure you have fruit and health bars available for those busier days. On the weekend, provide a variety of fresh food so that they can experiment with other healthy options.

Quiet Reading

Toddler Years

From the time my children were six months old, I have always had reading time straight after lunch. I simply wipe clean the highchair or place mat and pop out two to three books to read. I can then clean the kitchen uninterrupted. I start with about 5 minutes of reading time and build up to 15 minutes over the next six months.

The child is learning to focus and concentrate, to love books and is also developing the self-control to sit and read what, when and where he is told. Mum may also sit and read during this time to model that reading is important and for her own enjoyment. The skills gained during this time will transfer to doctor's waiting rooms, to watching older siblings at sporting events and to those long queues at the supermarket. I also focus on having my toddler read quietly during this time.

Teaching your toddler to control his voice and words is an enormous task for parents. Having him practice not talking for just a few minutes every day will greatly pay off in other situations during your week. I simply say it is reading time with no talking now and read my own book. At the end of the time I simply praise him for reading and eventually he learns that it is a quiet reading time.

School Years

Emily, Samuel and Caleb devoured many books each week during their school years. It was so rewarding to see them enjoying and pursuing such a worthwhile activity. Having reading time before school each day was an incentive for them to hurry through breakfast and making their lunch so they would have more time to read!

Make regular visits to the school or local library so that they have access to a wide variety of books and encourage them to read both fiction and non-fiction books. Chat to your friends to get ideas for good books. My three seemed to enjoy collecting and reading series of books and there are a few quality ones around, you just need to hunt for them among the plethora of sub-standard material available for this age group.

Teen Years

My teens received a new book for Easter, Christmas and their birthday each year. This was a straightforward way to encourage them to read. We would regularly discuss what we were reading so I was able to source books that matched their current interest or ones that I felt would stretch them.

Afternoon Nap or Rest

Toddler Years

All my children had an afternoon rest every day until they went to school. I think it is important that little ones have a break from the busyness of the house, from their siblings and from mum. It also gives them a chance to practice some self-control by staying quiet and on their bed for an hour.

Caleb actually slept every afternoon until he was five years old, while Emily and Sam stopped sleeping in the afternoons at around three years of age. When they stopped sleeping, I would simply give them a few picture books to look at or a couple of soft toys for the hour, as they still needed to rest.

One mother, who had three boys in three years, had a compulsory rest time each afternoon as it gave everyone a break. As soon as the boys could watch a clock, she popped a clock into their room and said they could get up when the big hand reach a certain point. If they got off their bed before that point, their rest time was increased. Very effective.

I looked forward to this time every day, particularly if we had had a busy morning. I would plan something fun for me like cross-stitch, reading, exercise, a long chat on the phone to a friend, quilting or simply resting. I have found this made my days at home more satisfying and this hour also refreshed me to cope with the rest of the day.

If you have a flexible pattern for your entire day, and you are making all the little decisions all day, your child will probably adjust to this expectation fairly quickly. You will also need to implement appropriate rewards for compliance and consequences for disobedience. More on that later.

School Years

In the early school years, I would ensure that my child had a rest time just before bed each evening. This enabled them to calm their body and minds and prepare for their night sleep. On the weekends, they would have an hour of quiet rest or reading time on their beds in the late afternoon. This gave them a break from siblings and ensured there was an hour of quiet in the house. During school holidays, they would have a rest hour straight after lunch each day and this was a welcome break for all to refresh and regroup after a busy morning together.

Teen Years

As I observe the teens I have been teaching for many years now, there seems to be two types in terms of rest. There are a few who are extra busy and involved in a myriad of activities and who also seem to be rushing to one thing or another.

The majority of these teens, however, seem to have fallen prey to idleness and are happy to waste many hours, even entire weekends or school holidays on mindless pursuits. Encouraging your teen to live a balanced life seems to be the key here, and this includes modelling to them how to rest well after work and responsibilities are completed.

Walk

Toddler Years

Most days I got out of the house to go for a walk. I safely secured my toddler in the pram and walked as fast as I could for my own exercise. The fresh air was good for us both and it was a good break from the house (especially if we had had a difficult morning).

My own physical need for exercise was being met each day and my toddler was also enjoying a change of scenery and could observe the flowers, cars and animals we saw along the way. While my toddler was also building a little more self-control by sitting in one place for the duration of the walk (getting out is simply not an option), a piece of fruit and a drink can also help pass this time. You may decide to meet up with a friend and walk together each day, and chat as you walk. This makes it more enjoyable and knowing someone is waiting for you also increases the chances of getting out for a walk each day.

When Caleb and Emily were only small (baby and toddler ages) I would put them in a double stroller and walk up and down our hilly Auckland suburb for 45 minutes each day. It was such good exercise that I even entered a 10km fun run and managed to finish the race. Having a goal to strive for motivated me to get out each day and it was also very satisfying to achieve my goal. Recently, I set the goal of completing a full 42 km marathon and was delighted to accomplish this last year.

School Years

Walk more! Walk to the shop together to pick up a few groceries. Walk to the nearest café for a treat together. Walk to the park to have a picnic on a sunny day. Walk to a field to play soccer, frisbee or chase. Enjoy being out in the fresh air, exercising and talking together.

Teen Years

Walk more! Walk as fast as you can together around a set route, and try and beat your previous time each week. Take a leisurely walk together to share an issue of the heart that requires some privacy away from listening siblings. Walk around the block to address an attitude or behaviour issue with your teen son. He is much more likely to be responsive if you have indirect eye contact and are distracted by doing something physical.

Free Play

Toddler Years

You may give your two or three-year-old a brief period each day to choose where and how he plays. This time should be between 30 and 60 minutes in length. Maybe give him a broad choice between outside play, toys in the lounge room or play in their room. He can choose what activity to do in each spot.

How your child plays during this time will be a good indication of how his self-control is developing. If he plays quietly and happily in one place and packs up after himself then he has obtained a good deal of self-control. If he runs around aimlessly and gets into things he shouldn't, then you know you have some work to do.

If he copes well with this freedom, then you can extend the time or give him two periods each day of free play. If he didn't cope very well, and 'messes' characterise this time, then simply shorten it to 10 or 20 minutes each day and slowly build it up again. Don't jump in too quickly. These times give you a chance to see how he is developing and help define what you need to work on.

One of my children coped very well with free play time from under two years, while another didn't cope at all until well after three years of age. I didn't despair, I just kept the rest of my day very tight, and made all the little decisions of the day until they slowly began to be characterised by more and more self-control. As school aged children, Caleb, Samuel and Emily generally made good choices and productively organised their time each day after school and for whole days during the school holidays.

School Years

My school aged children would have free play each afternoon after school. This was mostly outside play, weather permitting, of course. There were seasons where they played very well together out there. There were other seasons when they needed encouragement to play together nicely. (Isn't that a sweet way of saying they would argue constantly?) During the periods of discord, I would try and analyse the cause. If one child seemed to be the one who was causing the arguments, then they would have their free-time play inside for a week. If it was all of them who were contributing, then I would rotate them through time outside, time in their room and play in the lounge room for a week. After this week of mostly playing alone they were generally keen to play together again. Well, for a few weeks anyway.

Teen Years

Your teen will increasingly take ownership of their own weekly pattern. Their free time choices will show you what they value. If they prioritise time with their family and friends, then they are valuing relationships. If they are exclusively choosing to focus their free time on entertainment then they are worshipping pleasure. How your teen spends their free time will give you a window into their hearts that you will hopefully be able to discuss together.

Chores

Toddler Years

From my observation, it seems that many very young children love to help mum and dad with the household and outside chores. Make the most of this early interest.

By doing daily chores a child learns that she is an important member of a team, and that everyone has a vital part to play in the running of the household. She will learn not to sit back and expect to have everything done for her. A child learns to be responsible for her own tidiness, and of course she is practicing self-control as she does her little jobs happily and promptly each day.

As a parent, one of my goals for my children was that they would be able to completely manage a household by the time they were around fifteen years of age. I gradually trained them to clean, plan, shop, cook, prepare and follow a budget, handle repairs, wash and organise an entire house. Not only did I want them to know how to do these things; I wanted them to have enough self-discipline to do these things each and every day in a cheerful manner.

So, I began when they were very young and we worked on one thing at a time. For the first 1,000 days, it is actually much slower to have a toddler helping you but the early training will pay off over the next 10,000 days, so do persevere. You need to gradually raise the standard and be positive about all progress during this learning phase. Break each task into very small steps and be patient. This will be a very, very long process.

From about the time my child is one year old; I simply start by helping my child pack up the toys. Of course, it is mostly me who actually picks the toys up for the first few months, but by being consistent and calm, my child eventually follows suit. Have containers for each type of toy to help make clean up easier for your child.

From around 18 months of age I have my child help me with the sorting and folding of the washing. At first, he may just put each piece of clothing in the right pile. Then I will have him just fold the face cloths, then the shorts and so on, and slowly work away over the next few years until he can sort and fold every item of clothing. Having a five-year-old who can sort and put away the entire family washing is a great help.

Dusting, sweeping, wiping the table, wiping up (plastics only), raking or collecting leaves, getting the mail, putting out the rubbish, watering the plants, setting the table, baking cookies, putting soiled clothes in the washing basket, organising toys into piles, stripping beds, washing vegetables, cleaning their bike, washing the car etc., are all tasks that toddlers are capable of – with supervision.

Keep it positive and praise his success. If you are patient he will eventually get to your standard. Do it with him and explain first. Always show your appreciation for his effort and his attitude. Give ownership to the tasks (for example, 'Caleb helps keep our car washed and clean'). Redo any tasks discreetly and without ridiculing your toddler's efforts.

At age four, Sam learnt to wipe down the placemats after a meal. He did it every day and I simply expected him to do his bit to contribute to the family. At first, we focused on showing him how to wipe and how to put the cloth away tidily.

I praised him for being a good helper and while he was off brushing his teeth, I quickly wiped them again. He would never learn if I didn't let him practice or if I was negative toward his early effort. As it became his daily habit (doing it without prompting) I worked towards him cleaning the place mats adequately.

Doing chores together was one of the nicest times of the day for my children. We were all working together and they were being positively affirmed for their efforts and attitudes. I think their genuine contribution to the family also gave them a keen sense of belonging and a feeling of importance. The repeated explanations and patience required in the initial stages were rewarded many times over.

School Years

These are the training years. Your aim over the next few years is to gradually teach your child how to complete every household chore. In your family, you may have a daily, weekly or monthly rotating system for chores, or you may allocate chores for the whole term. Any system that works for you is fine. You want your child to learn how to complete the chore to an acceptable standard and to be able to complete them without prompting each day.

Teen Years

These are the fruitful years. During these years, your child will take over entire areas of responsibility. For example, as teens, my children were totally responsible for cleaning their own bathroom, vacuuming the entire house, dusting, emptying the rubbish, completing their own washing and ironing and caring for their own room. In addition, they each had one night per week in which to prepare, serve and clean up a family meal. Delightful!

Television Time

Toddler Years

A brief time each day in front of a carefully selected television show or children's video has many advantages. By sitting still to concentrate solely on the program, and not just catching glimpses of a show as they wander around, your child is learning to focus and concentrate. Once again it is an opportunity to build a little more self-control into your toddler's life. Your child is also able to learn from and enjoy the program.

Don't allow the television to be on continuously. Excessive background noise is distracting both to your toddler's ability to concentrate on his play and to his ability to hear and respond to your instructions. A quiet and orderly environment will greatly enhance your child's day.

Having your toddler watching happily and staying in one place, enables a parent to get a few chores done in the late afternoon, like bringing the clothes in off the line, chopping some vegetables or squeezing in a quick phone call. If you have a younger child you can pop him securely in his highchair in front of the television. Some mums give their child afternoon tea then to help stretch them out to the 20 or 30 minutes of the whole program.

For an older toddler, ensure you have him sit in a small chair or on a mat. Be very specific. You do not want him rolling around or walking all over the lounge room. If he chooses not to sit and watch, then he simply sits on his bed for the duration of the program. Sam tended to get hyperactive when he was tired and started to run around and get loud. Popping him in front of a show for a brief 20 or 30 minutes helped him to get his body a little more under control.

We found a Character Building video series very appropriate for the toddler age group. Sitting and watching a little story on patience or kindness greatly helped my teaching of those virtues at other times of the day. My two and three-year-old just loved the little songs on these videos too, and hearing my little one singing about the importance of obedience or politeness was such a delight.

School Years

Generally, my school aged children had no TV shows during the week. Of course, there were the odd exceptions for a special event which they greatly appreciated. On the weekend, they had an hour on Saturday morning if they were home and often watched a children's movie on Saturday or Sunday night. The day was filled with a balance of other activities so the time for just sitting and watching was limited.

Teen Years

During this stage, there did seem to be a show on most nights that someone wanted to watch. On the weekend, sporting events were an enjoyed viewing choice. In the early teen years, I would generally ask them to fulfil their responsibilities before watching. In the later teen years, this was an area of freedom for which they could take responsibility.

Bath

Toddler Years

I get many emails from mums asking me how anyone can manage to cook dinner, bath a toddler, feed a toddler, deal with a cranky toddler and their own tiredness, and eat and enjoy their own dinner.

It is a difficult part of the day to manage. However, it can run smoothly with a little practice. Your routine over the rest of the day will greatly influence the success of this phase of your day. If you are struggling with this hour or two, then tighten up your routine and ensure you are making all the little decisions throughout the day for your toddler. There are a few ways to organise this time and I will share one plan with you.

I have always bathed my toddlers around 4:00 pm in the afternoon. This avoids the rush and stress of trying to squeeze it in either just before dinner, when you are busy preparing the evening meal, or the time straight after dinner when your toddler is very tired and cranky, ready for bed and far less likely to be cooperative.

Make the most of the time when your toddler is in the bath. You can either make it a positive teaching time by practicing a kindness rhyme, a memory verse or an obedience song. Or, depending on the layout of your bathroom, use the time to clean the bathroom. As long as your toddler is always in view, you can use this time to clean your shower, sink and toilet without having your toddler underfoot. Safety must be ensured.

School Years

By the time your child starts school, they should be able to adequately bathe themselves and wash their own hair each day.

Teen Years

Please ensure that your teen is bathing daily. So many do not and it is most unpleasant to be in a closed classroom with them. Also, do instruct them on the need for more frequent hair washing to counteract the extra grease produced by their hormones.

Table Play

Toddler Years

While I was preparing the evening meal I had my toddler up at the dinner table seated in his highchair or strapped into his booster seat (depending on his age). My toddler was not touching things he shouldn't or getting dangerously underfoot in the kitchen.

He could clearly see me and we could chat as I cooked and he played. He was also not being bothered by, or bothering, his siblings. My toddler was practicing self-control and I could quickly get dinner prepared and on the table without any 'messes' occurring throughout the house. Choose simple activities that will amuse your toddler and that don't require any assistance or preparation from you. Some suggested activities include: drawing on one piece of paper with a crayon, one or two cars or trucks to drive on the highchair tray or place mat, two or three plastic cups, a small chalk board and a piece of chalk, one doll, a couple of plastic animals to move about, magnetic letters, a few building blocks, a toy with lots of buttons, a container of pegs or similar put in and out, a wooden puzzle, stacking cups or rings, dominoes, a 'Where's Wally?' type book for young children, fuzzy felts, activity books, a mixing bowl and spoon to copy mummy, Playdoh, pegboard, or threading activities.

As you implement a routine into your week, you will find that your toddler can sit and play for increasingly longer periods of time. Keep your meals simple during this initial stage so that your toddler will only be sitting for a very brief time and you can encourage his effort through praise.

This time will change into homework time once your child is at school and the valuable skills learnt throughout the toddler and pre-school years will ensure a smooth transition. Each night I was in the kitchen preparing dinner and answering questions, helping with spelling words or testing times table answers for my older two. Sam was also busily doing his own 'homework' or playing quietly at the table. It was a pleasant family time and very peaceful.

It is challenging work initially to be preparing dinner and teaching your toddler to sit for table play at the same time, but if you keep it short and positive you will reap the benefits. On days where Caleb couldn't quite stretch out to dinner I would give him a small piece of fruit or a drink for the last few minutes.

School Years

Your school aged child will use the skills developed during the toddler years to sit and work quietly while you have your hair or nails done, while you are waiting in a medical room or for an appointment of any kind, when you are in a café or restaurant, when you are visiting friends who do not have children, while watching a sibling's game, concert or performance, and while sitting in church. There are many times when the skills of sitting and working quietly will be beneficial for you and your child.

Teen Years

Many of the teens I teach really struggle with the self-control to study each evening. Even with the best intentions they are distracted by a myriad of things and fail to sit and focus for the hours required in senior study. Training your toddler, and then school aged child, to sit and concentrate is a valuable gift that you can give your teen that will maximise their potential academic success.

Dinner

Toddler Years

As much as possible we would try to sit down together as a family for dinner. If I had had a very bad day then I would move dinner forward and put everyone to bed early and enjoy a quiet kid-free meal after that. However, most days we would eat together.

At dinner time, the focus would be on talking to each other and not on the food. As we ate, the adults would have their own special talking time first. This provided an opportunity to catch up on each other's day, any interesting news or current affairs, and the highlights of the children's day. As we talked, the children were eating their own meals and so we rarely had slow eaters to deal with. After five or ten minutes, we then included the whole family in the conversation.

Be very careful not to get into bad habits. You cannot make your child eat. Food can be a very powerful and emotive weapon for a toddler. Refusing to eat, or eating very slowly can evoke a very strong reaction in mum and dad and is very effective for gaining attention.

I gave my children very small amounts of food and then praised them for trying it. They could always ask for more. I did not focus on what they were eating or the speed they were eating at. After a reasonable time, I simply cleared the plates without any comment on what was or was not eaten. Those who ate all their dinner received dessert.

I didn't coax or give second or tenth chances. Having the dessert in the middle of the table can be a very strong non-verbal incentive. This way dinner is peaceful and the child eventually learns that it pays to eat their dinner.

Sam, at two years of age, was eating one bean and two carrots with his meal (he had no trouble eating meat, pasta or potatoes). He had no afternoon tea so we were sure he had a good appetite for dinner. Most nights we had fruit for dessert. If he ate his vegetables he got dessert, if he didn't then he sat at the table and missed out, and if he complained, he sat on his bed until dinner was over.

Emily is quite slim and has always had a very small appetite. She would only eat a few mouthfuls of food at each meal yet she was still happy and full of energy all day. She ate very little of a variety of foods. Caleb has always had a larger appetite and eats good platefuls of a variety of foods. So, you can cater for your toddler's uniqueness, and still ensure they are getting adequate nutrition, without it dominating the evening meal.

This approach will only work if your child is characterised by self-control in other areas of their day. The other typical mealtime 'messes' of a toddler will also be minimised by an orderly day of structured play. Once you have established a calm and orderly evening meal you can add some variety to your meal. Eat on an outside table or have an indoor picnic. Have a theme night with dress ups too. Go out for dessert or eat dessert first.

On Sunday night, my children loved watching a family show while eating cheese on toast on a picnic rug. Even as toddlers they could enjoy this treat because of their self-control. There were no spills for me to deal with as they sat still and watched. It was a lovely way to end the weekend.

School Years

Let the focus of dinner during these years be social skills. Teach them questions they can ask about each other's day. Teach them how to provide one piece of information and then direct the conversation to another person. Show them how to listen carefully and ask a further question about what was shared. Model how to include quieter individuals into the conversation. Explain how to respond appropriately to the news that is shared in a manner that shows care and empathy. These skills will greatly help them in other social situations.

Teen Years

Let the focus of dinner during these years be thoughtful discussions. Ask them to summarise a current affair. Encourage them to express their opinion on a hot issue and to provide an explanation for that opinion. Model how to segue into a new topic of conversation. Practise having debates on current issues, as this will help them provide reasoned arguments for their opinion. Show them how to disagree with respect and how to work to understand an opposing viewpoint. This will greatly assist their essay writing tasks and debating skills at school and their communication skills in their future ministry and vocation pursuits.

Family Play

Toddler Years

Family play is simply a time when the family is together. The aim is just to enjoy each other and some fun activities. It is a chance to focus on the importance and uniqueness of your family. It can last 20 minutes or an hour, depending on the activity or the circumstances of the day. Be creative and choose things that each member of your family can participate in.

Watching a video together, reading a book out loud, playing a board game, charades, hide-n-seek, sock wrestling, tickles, looking through photo albums, talking about your own childhood, going for a walk, going out for ice cream, or playing with a favourite toy are a few suggestions. Or make up your own story with each person adding a line or two (with sound effects), toddlers love it and come up with some classic lines!

School Years

Parents have shared that Family Time is a bit more challenging with both little ones and school aged children to cater for. One family with six children have fish and chips for dinner, followed by a game that the little ones enjoy. Then the little ones are put to bed and the parents and the older children can play a board game more suited to them. Another family went on a search for family movies that appeal to a wide audience and that became their staple family night for that season.

Teen Years

Parents have shared that finding a regular night for the family to get together with teens who have musical and sports practice, larger study commitments, part-time jobs and church activities, as well as their social schedule, is quite challenging. One family of four has dinner together early on Sunday evening each week, and aims for a fun family activity once a month. Another family of seven children spend Sunday morning bushwalking or exploring or picnicking together and they attend church in the evening.

Bedtime

Toddler Years

Have a ritual for bed preparation. Do the same things in the same order at the same time every night. Each family will be different, just think through a routine that will fit for you. You may have a routine of teeth, drink, toilet, reading, talking with mum or dad, prayers and then lights out.

I always asked my children if they would like to read their Bibles for 10 minutes or have lights out. For some reason, they have always chosen to read. This helped them quiet down and develops a habit that will last all through their lives. We also had the same peaceful music tape playing each night to signal that it was time for sleep.

With the lights out, I would chat for just a few minutes with each child about the day or any concerns they had – it was a positive time, we did not discuss any behaviour issues here. We ended the day on a positive note with a quick prayer and then a hug and kiss goodnight.

If your child is currently going to bed at 9:00 pm or 10:00 pm then you may want to bring it back slowly. Aim for a 9:30 pm bedtime for a few days and then 9:00 pm for the next few days and so on. You will work back until you are somewhere between 6:30 pm and 8:00 pm for your toddler's bedtime.

As you work on self-control during your entire day, you will find that bedtime becomes very peaceful and predictable.

You will then be able to enjoy time to yourself each evening to relax, chat with your spouse and friends, or pursue your own hobby.

Your toddler will be well-rested for the next day and you will be refreshed.

School Years

Keep having the same bedtime each night during the school years. Having the eldest in bed by 8:00 pm with lights out at 8:30 pm will provide them with the sleep they need for maximum performance during the day. Staggering the sleep times from youngest to oldest will ensure you can have 5 – 10 minutes with each child just before they go to sleep.

It is during this time that they will often share the issues that are weighing on their hearts. Be gentle. If you listen carefully and empathise with these tender little heartaches, they will trust you to share their bigger issues in the years to come.

Teen Years

In the early teen years, the bedtime was kept to being in bed by 9:00 pm with lights out by 9.30pm. This ensured they could get to school on time. For their senior years of school and university study they needed to be up much later. I gave the general guideline of being in bed before midnight. During these later years, it was a delight to my heart when they would come to me for a late-night chat and share their hearts.

12

Motivating Behaviour

How do you think our children should respond to our requests and directions regarding their behaviour?

Well, personally I think they should reply, 'Oh mother dear, you are so wonderful. I greatly appreciate all the amazing sacrifices you make just for me. Out of my undying love and gratitude for you, of course I will obey you quickly and happily, this time and every time.'

Unfortunately, this is not reality. Most young children do not respond to reasoning (for example, 'Eat your beans because they are nutritious') nor do they respond to 'No', or even a loud 'No'.

Toddlers respond to concrete consequences. These consequences can be positive or negative. For example, a huge cheer and a hug for packing up the toys, or no dessert for not eating the vegetables, or a small treat for visiting the bathroom, all motivate behaviour. If your consequences are calmly and consistently applied, then you will see positive changes.

Over time.

If you have a very stubborn child it is vitally important that you are (outwardly) calm when you are responding to their difficult behaviour. These children love getting an emotional outburst from mum and will often keep pushing until you explode. Consistently respond the first time to their behaviour and have a very firm consequence. Do not let them control the environment in the family.

Each of my children was born self-pleasing and lacking in self-control (though absolutely gorgeous too!) and all questioned and pushed the boundaries. However, one in particular was very stubborn. This particular child took longer to achieve self-control in most parts of their day. This child also required much stronger positive and negative consequences for change to occur.

My longest battle with this child, from around two years of age, was over squealing when bothered or frustrated. Many, many reminders to say 'No, thanks' or 'Help, please' in those moments were given. Positive rewards were offered every time verbal self-control was shown. A calm, negative consequence was given every time verbal self-control was not shown. I was consistent.

We role-played and talked through scenarios in our focus play each morning. Our day was structured and I was making all the little decisions of the day. Over six months we went from 30 squeals an hour to about 3 a day. Some days were worse than others, and some weeks I felt we were going backwards. I did have times of despair. Things were, however, gradually improving and over time we saw results.

I share this story with you to encourage you. Some children are harder to parent than others. Some children do just love to be awkward and seem to almost enjoy 'bucking the system'. But do not lose heart, you can build positive virtues into all their little hearts over time. Do remember it is often the difficult child that has the most delightful personality, so do persevere and enjoy the emergence of their special uniqueness.

Sometimes you will be working on a situation for only an hour or two, sometimes a couple of days, or maybe even for a few months. You will need to increase the intensity of the consequences over this time.

If you are dealing with the same issue over and over, then progressively increase the consequence. Maybe change your consequence, or combine it with another. The consequence needs to promote or deter a particular behaviour. Also note that each child will respond differently to various consequences. What worked with your first child will probably be ineffective for your second.

For example, what reason does an 18-month-old child have for wearing a sun hat? Parents will have cognitive reasons for expecting this behaviour. However, explaining the damaging effects of the sun's rays on the skin to an 18-month-old child will not be effective. An appropriate concrete consequence, that is calmly and consistently applied, will be motivating. One child may respond to a light squeeze on the hand every time the hat is pulled at, while another child will respond to verbal praise.

Think through situations from your toddler's viewpoint. Why would they obey?

School Years

The best time to talk to your child about their behaviour is in non-emotional times when they are well-rested and well-fed. The moment of conflict and high emotion is not an effective time to talk to them. They will not hear your words through the wall of heightened emotion. During these calm times, keep your talk to less than five minutes. Clearly state the issue and the consequence. Do not nag and go on and on. They simple tune you out.

In the moment of the behaviour, have your child move to the same place each time. I would have them sit on their bed. When they were calm, they would fill out their life lessons book. This was just a blank book in which they independently answered these four questions:

- What did I do wrong?
- Why is it wrong?
- What will I do to make it right?
- What will I do next time?

Writing this out helped the child own the behaviour and saved me repeating myself over and over. Your consequence needs to be focused on the loss of freedoms and privileges and needs to be progressive. So, for example, if two were arguing over the computer game, they would lose the freedom of playing it for a week. The next time they would lose it for two weeks, then three and so on.

Teen Years

In the early teen years, you will need to be sharing the positive fruits that come from positive choices. Comment on this when you see good in the news or in others, and be quick to draw attention to their own choices. Ask them how they feel when they do good things. When we do right we feel right and that is a powerful motivation for choosing right behaviour. Have firm boundaries and consistent consequences if they choose to challenge those boundaries. If previously they lost a freedom for a week then two weeks, now have them lose it for a month, then two months. This is your last season of being able to guide them towards the right path so stay firm and finish strong.

When your older teen makes unwise choices, and they all do, you will need to allow them to experience the natural consequence of that choice, even though you will desperately long to jump in and rescue or minimise the damage. All teens need to learn that choices have an impact on themselves and others, and some teens will only learn when they experience the full weight of these choices. Let them fail an assessment task if they choose not to hand it in on time, let them choose how to spend their first pay from their part-time job, let them miss out on social events with their friends. Or if they choose not to work, let them deal with not having the right clothes on the right day if they have chosen not to wash their clothes on the weekend, and have them pay their own fines for speeding or to repeat an academic course they fail.

The teens at school who have parents who are constantly rescuing them from the reality of their choices are immature, have a poor attitude and are characterised by expectations of entitlement. The teens who are learning to take responsibility for their choices are mature, pleasant and resilient. They know that their choices have implications and they are developing into responsible citizens who are a delight to be with.

Philippians 3:12 'Not that I have already obtained all this, or have already arrived at my goal, but I press on to take hold of that for which Christ Jesus took hold of me.'

We read Mel's books very early on in our parenting journey starting with the first one when Bec was about 12 months. So, we implemented as much as possible right from the beginning. As often happens with a first born we were quite diligent and intentional. I remember one day, after a picnic in a park when Bec was about 2½ and it was time to go, Bec threw the biggest most embarrassing tantrum and we had to carry her screaming to the car. My husband was mortified that it had happened and said, 'What is the point of doing all this stuff, if we still end up with this behaviour?'

The thing is our daughter was not perfect, in fact she was quite normal, but I felt empowered by the fact that I knew what to do with her when she threw her fit. We carried her to the car, strapped her into her seat and sat on the kerb and waited for her to get self-control. Once she calmed down, we told her that was unacceptable behaviour and there would be a consequence when we got home. Then we got in the car, drove home and followed through with the consequence and she apologised. I can't say that was the only time that that sort of thing happened but incidents like that were few and far between.

Now 14 years later, she has amazing self-control, and we have a wonderful relationship where she will talk to us and we can communicate in a way that is respectful, humble and polite. However, if any of us do 'lose' it (and we do sometimes) we are usually quick to apologise and restore the relationship. Through all the ups and downs of life, I am so grateful for the relationship I have with my daughter, the foundations of which started back in the very early years by implementing the information that we learnt in the Terrific Toddler Books.

Cathy, Mum to 2

Sometimes we don't balance! But tomorrow is a new day! Life has a pattern, but it's a pattern, not a firm road. Things change along the way, patterns can slightly vary. We need to teach our kids that a road ahead is good but we need to be able to accept the variations in the pattern. Being flexible means we are kind and accepting. It's usually towards others where we need flexibility and an inability to be flexible is actually teaching selfishness.

Kate, Mum to 2

13

Implementation

So, how do you implement a flexible pattern into your day?

Write out the hours in a day down one side of the page. On the right side of your page or screen you will write out your schedule and on the left you will write out your toddler's schedule. Put in your meal and morning/afternoon tea times first, then sleep or rest times. Put in the blocks of time you need to do household chores. I'm not a great housekeeper so I tend to get everything done as quickly as I can in three blocks; you may need more time or less.

From here, you have two choices. You can either plan to balance the rest of your day with a mixture of quiet and busy activities. Or you can work through each of the needs for you and your toddler (physical, emotional, social, spiritual and intellectual) and plan fun activities that will meet each of those needs. You do not want to neglect your child all day, nor do you want her demanding your attention all day. Find a healthy balance between these two extremes.

Plan:
- Activities that are done with you (for example, an educational learning time);
- Activities that are done near you (for example, table play while you are completing some chores); and
- Activities that are done without you (for example, room play or outside play). This balance is especially important when you have more than one child.

Be sure to take your child's individuality into account. Is she happier in the morning or the afternoon? Is she active or more sedate? Does she enjoy craft or music? Is she an indoor or outdoor person? Is she very social or does she prefer to play alone?

You will not totally cater to your child's preferences, but you will lean towards them. For example, all children should be exposed to books from an early age, but your child may be particularly attracted to books, so may have two or three different reading opportunities each day. She could have a time to read alone, a time of being read to by mum, an audio story to listen to or a computer story to watch each day.

Aim for most activities to last 30 minutes. A few will be planned for 15 minutes and others (for example outside play) may last an hour. Remember that you determine the length of each activity, not your child. Try to gradually increase the length of each activity as your child develops more and more self-control. Your two-year-old may be able to focus for 20 or 30 minutes on one activity, whereas your three-year-old may be able to sit and concentrate for 40 or 50 minutes.

Print out your routine, pin it in a prominent place in your house and try it out. Be positive and excited about each activity and have small treats for your child as they comply. Expect them to enjoy this new day, and focus on the fun aspect of each activity. Praise all the good you see and try and ignore the not so good (just for these first few days).

Include pictures on your chart to describe the activity. This gives you and your child a visual reminder of the order of your day. Most toddlers love looking at the pictures on the chart and working out what the next activity for the day will be.

Put all but your essential chores on hold for a few days. Plan quick and easy meals for dinner. Be available to hover around each activity to encourage and motivate your child. Then evaluate at the end of each day. What parts flowed well? What part was a total disaster? What improvements have you seen since yesterday? Should you change any parts or give it a few more days to settle down?

Focus on the positive. If your daughter played in her room by herself for 20 minutes – praise her. You may have been hoping for 30 minutes, but 20 minutes is still very good for a first day. Remember it will take between three days and three weeks for you to see a total change in your household.

What do you do if you are working towards 20 minutes of reading time after lunch and your child will only read for 10 minutes? Praise them for reading so quietly and then simply read to them for the last part. At least they will still be sitting and you can gradually increase their quiet reading time over the next few weeks.

What do you do if your child wants to come in half-way through outside play? Go and play outside with her. Tomorrow you can stretch her out a few extra minutes and within a very short time you will be enjoying an hour to yourself and your toddler will have also learnt to enjoy herself outside fully for that time too.

Some mums may think about implementing one new activity at a time into their toddler's day. This is not very successful for mum or toddler. Thirty minutes of structure and self-control training in the morning will be greatly overshadowed by an entire day of choices and freedom. I would suggest you aim to implement structure into your entire day from the beginning. Although this is very hard work for the first week, you will see a huge change relatively quickly. This is because it is the environment of orderly calm that is so helpful in teaching self-control, and each activity will help the next activity. The self-control it takes to sit and do a puzzle will aid your teaching of sitting and focusing during table play later in the day, or eating quietly at the dinner table.

Reread the chapters on the advantages for parent and toddler of a flexible routine each morning and night during this first week. Keep fresh in your mind what you are working toward. Be excited. You are working on the cause of toddler 'messes' and not just the symptoms.

Outlined here are two sample days for a mum with one toddler.

Sample Routine 1

Child	Parent
Breakfast	
Television	Shower, Washing, Bathroom
Focus Play	
Outside Play	Cleaning, Tidying, Extra Jobs
Lunch	
Sleep/Rest	Craft, Read, Relax, Hobby
Free Play	
Table Play	
Outside Play	Washing, Phone, Extra Jobs
Room Play	Dinner Prep
Dinner and Bath	
Family Play and Bed	Craft, Read, Relax, Hobby

Sample Routine 2

Child	Parent
Breakfast	
Room Play	Shower, Washing, Bathroom
Focus Play and Puzzle Time	
Outside Play	Cleaning, Tidying, Extra Jobs
Lunch and Quiet Reading	
Sleep/Rest	Craft, Read, Relax, Hobby
Walk and Free Play	
Chores	
Television	Washing, Phone, Extra Jobs
Bath	
Table Play	Dinner Prep
Dinner	
Family Play	
Bed	Craft, Read, Relax, Hobby

A weekly outline may look like this:

MONDAY	Day at home
TUESDAY	Mum's Group or Play Group
WEDNESDAY	Day at home
THURSDAY	Kindy gym or Tiny Tots Music Class Friend over for lunch
FRIDAY	Day at home
SATURDAY & SUNDAY	Shopping & Visiting Friends Church and Family Day

School Years

For the school years, we had a weekly pattern that was quite stable, while the weekends were quite changeable. The daily schedule included meals, chores, school homework, sport and music practice and quiet, family and sibling play times. I would type out the weekly schedule and pop it on the fridge so everyone could see which activity was on which day. Having your morning and afternoon schedule there on the fridge is a great visual prompt for your child, so they can check and then do the next thing they need to do.

Teen Years

My young teens would write out their own weekly pattern and bring it to me for checking. By this stage, they knew to include a daily chores time, homework hour, outside activity time, family time and a reasonable bedtime. If they had hopes for a new extra-curricular event, we would talk through the practicality of adding that, or replacing it with a current activity. By the mid-teens, they would independently organise and follow their own weekly pattern, with varying degrees of aptitude. Successful people always plan and my desire was that they would be successful in the journey of life, regardless of their chosen career path.

Titus 1:8 'Rather he must be hospitable, one who loves what is good, who is self-controlled, upright, holy and disciplined.'

14

More than One

Is it possible to have a calm and orderly day when you have more than one child? Whether you have two children or five, from toddler age and up, or a toddler and a newborn, you can work toward a balanced week that helps meet the needs of every member of your family.

You will be able to avoid many of the toddler 'messes' and care for a baby, if your baby is on a flexible feeding pattern. The DVD *Babywise Bliss*, provides excellent practical advice regarding the care and nurture of your newborn. *Calm Baby, Confident Mum* is the best Australian book I've found to help manage those precious first few months.

If you do have a baby and a toddler, you will need to write out your baby's feeding pattern first. Then write your own plan for your chores and needs, followed by the pattern for your toddler's day. Try and have this new pattern in place a month or two before your baby arrives. This gives you a chance to iron out this new pattern and ensure you have regular 30 minute times to feed your baby throughout the day. It also means that your toddler's day will be almost uninterrupted on baby's arrival. This will greatly help your toddler to accept the new addition.

Be flexible, and adjust your pattern to meet the changing needs of your baby as he or she grows. In that first year of having a two-year-old and a baby, my pattern seemed to change every six weeks or so. I was constantly changing it as my baby had longer periods between feeds and changed nap times.

If you have three or more children, you simply will not be able to have an individual schedule for each child. You will need to do almost everything together. The children will all have table play at the same time – the little ones will have small toys, while the older ones may have a craft to do. For TV time, you may have the use of two sets to show age appropriate videos at the same time, or have an older child use the computer then. During outside play the older ones may have the freedom to play out the front of your house (depending on safety, of course) while the younger ones are playing in the backyard.

You may find that a weekly plan works best for you. Rather than trying to fit every activity into each day, you may plan to have some activities only two or three times over a week. For example, you may divide focus play time into craft one day, baking the next, singing one day and pre-school academics on the other two days. This can be a lot easier than trying to bake, sing and teach each day.

The greatest challenge will be working out how to have focus play with each child. The day time sleeps or earlier bedtime of the younger child can be a good chance to focus on an older one. Taking one child on an errand with you and stopping for a snack and a chat is another idea (if your partner, friend or relative is minding the other children, of course).

One creative mother of four would have a rotating hour in her day. Each child would have 15 minutes with mum, 15 minutes on the computer, 15 minutes doing puzzles and 15 minutes of play in the family room. They would then all have morning tea together and spend the rest of the morning playing outside.

Stay positive and keep implementing a daily schedule until you find one that works for you. Talk with other families who are also proactively planning out their week to provide an optimal environment for their family. Share ideas with each other. I was constantly improving my day, sometimes in response to the changing needs of my children, sometimes in response to our current family situation, and sometimes just for a bit of variety. Plan a day that your children enjoy, and that you enjoy too.

School Years

Many of the parents I speak to share that they find it realistic to aim for a weekly time with each child during this season. Sometimes this is on the way home from a sport or music practice during the week, other times it may be while watching a sibling practice dance or drama. One mum chose to have daily one-to-one time with her toddler during the day, with her six-year-old over afternoon tea and with her nine-year-old when the younger two were in bed for the night. Another mum had one child accompany her for the grocery shopping each Saturday morning and they enjoyed a morning tea treat on the way. Be creative and find something that works for you.

Teen Years

Enjoying common interests is a fun part of having teens. Sam and I would often play table tennis together in the evenings. We kept a running tally of the winner each time. Caleb and I would play tennis together. We would both run lots and end up sweating profusely as we played long, close games we both enjoyed. We also enjoyed watching major sporting events together, mostly soccer matches. Emily and I both love to watch musical productions, so we would enjoy low budget local productions regularly, with one major performance seen each year. Over the last few Summers, we have all enjoyed finding new beaches around our city to go snorkelling. These opportunities create fun times and great memories.

Psalm 127:4-5 'Like arrows in the hands of a warrior are children born in one's youth. How joyful is the man whose quiver is full of them.'

> *We have one child who has a bent towards a lack of self-control with a low pain threshold. If he were to complain of a sore ear – I would tend to say – 'You'll be right' and sure enough he generally would be – don't get me wrong if it persisted I would get it checked out. . . We have another child who has a much higher pain threshold and if he complained of a sore ear – I would be rushing him to emergency, probably with a burst ear drum. . . Now as teenagers they both have learnt to speak up at the appropriate times.*

Our child with a lack of self-control was hard work but the hard work paid off in the long run. All through his life we have talked about this character trait in many positive ways to encourage him to attain more self-control. At many times, we were disheartened about whether we were getting anywhere, but grandparent visits approximately once a year often gave us encouragement. They would often say each time they came, 'Wow, he has come a long way, we remember last time we were here, he would do this. . .' As were in the thick of it, we often forgot how far we had come and that there was some progress in the year, even if it didn't seem like it to us. This wasn't to say we could stop working on it as we still had a long way to go.

Now as a teenager he understands what a lack of self-control looks like, knows he has a bent towards it, and continues to work on it himself with some coaching from us when necessary. He has learnt from the moral training we have done and having a way of escape when he finds himself tempted in the wrong way is extremely helpful.

Alicia, Mum to 4

15

Parental Model

Model – representation of proposed structure; person or thing proposed for display or imitation; give shape to; exemplify.

Our own behaviour will greatly influence our child's behaviour. If we desire our child to be kind, helpful, cheerful, patient and loving, then we must be displaying those virtues ourselves first. This thought is quite sobering, isn't it?

Our own words, actions, attitudes, priorities, choices, and beliefs are all being transferred daily to our child. This sometimes occurs directly through speech, but more often it is simply taught through long-term daily observation.

If we are loud and impatient in our speech, then our child will mimic that form. For a time, I had regular contact with a mother who would yell and swear at her daughter as the standard pattern of interaction. From around 2 ½ years of age the daughter would yell and swear back at her mother, using exactly the same phrases and volume. It was very sad.

At times, Emily, as a toddler, would speak a little impatiently to her brothers or start speaking quite crossly to her dolls. I would often be the cause of this, speaking in a frustrated or short tone towards my children. By simply adjusting my speech, I would notice a remarkable corresponding improvement in my daughter's words. One day I overheard Caleb, maybe just three, sighing at his younger sister and saying, 'I've told you four hundred, and seventy-three hundred times not to do that.' I wonder where that phrase came from?

Your child will also be noting your attitudes towards everything including other people, nutrition, authority, exercise, money, wealth, animals, queues and crowds, daily interruptions, other drivers, and so on, and these attitudes all contribute to character building.

The purpose of your life may be to focus on fun and enjoyment, serving others, pleasing yourself, building spiritual treasure, wealth or comfort or a mixture of these or others. You may be striving through life progressively realising the goals you periodically set, or you may be meandering through from year to year. The purpose of your life may be articulated or unspoken. Either way, it will be influencing your child.

The quote – 'Don't tell me what you believe in, tell me what you do, and I'll tell you what you believe in', is very true. What does your lifestyle say about your life purpose? A frantic rushing from event to event in a daily atmosphere of clutter and chaos is not conducive to effective parenting. Neither is an obsession with household cleanliness. However, a calm and orderly environment, that enables you to patiently respond to your child's behaviour, will greatly facilitate your toddler's character development. And it's more fun too!

Parents also model their perspective on dealing with conflict. Some cope with conflict by avoiding or ignoring differences of opinion on various issues. Others approach it by yelling and attacking the other person, and then moving on as if nothing has happened. If, however, parents accept conflict as a part of life and seek to understand and constructively resolve issues, then you can be sure the young child will also reflect that attitude.

As parents, we are not perfect models to our children. We all have times of frustration and impatience. We have good days and not so good days. That is very normal. We are not aiming for impossible perfection. Rather, we should aim for excellence in our parenting.

Our own model does not excuse or prevent our child's negative behaviour, but it is often a key ingredient to consider in virtue training. For example, if your toddler is messy, angry or impatient, you first need to ask yourself, 'Am I also characterised by this behaviour?' By striving to be tidy, even-tempered and patient yourself, you will definitely set the best foundation for then correcting the negatives and enhancing the positives.

What areas of your parental model can you improve on?

School Years

During these years, you are modelling how to respond in many new and different situations. These include how to be a good friend in the playground, how to listen to the sports or music teacher, how to behave as a visitor, how to act in church, how to host a birthday party, how to lose without excuse and how to win without boasting, how to handle not being invited to that birthday party, how to take turns, how to express extreme emotions in an acceptable manner, how to celebrate, how to respect a decision the teacher has made and a myriad of other life experiences. Be there with your child and explain the practical and ethical reasons behind the expected responses and choices. Encourage them to choose well.

Teen Years

Teens see us with new eyes. They clearly identify where our talk does not match our walk and this can be quite humbling to hear. Your influence here comes through relationship and the opportunities you will have to talk through the issues they are facing. Your model of over-spending, budgeting wisely or saving excessively will be noted. Your own attitude to unfair decisions and difficult people in your workplace will impact how your teen chooses to respond to their own work situation and the difficult personalities there. If you live for entertainment and fleeting pleasure and spend the week planning for the weekend thrill, your teen will see that just as clearly as seeing a disciplined life that manages time well and still plans times of rest and relaxation. Live well yourself and be available for discussions.

Titus 2:7 'In everything set them an example by doing what is good. In your teaching, show integrity.'

16

Daily Life

Daily – on every day; from day to day; constantly.

Life – state of functional activity and continual change peculiar to organised matter.

Our toddler is learning all day every day, whether we plan for it or not, and, at times, whether we want it to be happening or not. Little eyes are always watching our behaviour, little ears are always listening to our conversations and a little heart is being touched day by day.

Is the washing done in a resentful, hostile manner, perceived as just another chore for the day, or is it viewed as an opportunity to please people we love? Does the toddler see mum giving generously of her time through baby-sitting, or doing odd jobs, or preparing meals for others, and graciously handling interruptions? Is the home filled with angry voices and frustrated, repeated threats or the calm, but firm, logical and consistent responses to inappropriate behaviour?

Do mum and dad speak kindly to each other, take a little time to chat and focus only on each other, every day, or are they distant and cold toward each other? Is gym class or music group attended every week without fail while church attendance is occasional? Is the television the focus of the family routine, a constant background noise, or is it only reserved for quality selected programs?

Does the toddler receive an 'I love you' every day? Is mum happy to take time out each day from the household chores and simply play?

Priorities and values are being formed through all of these observations and interactions, and many others. Training values into the hearts of our child is mostly secondary to the task that is tangible.

For example, bath time is obviously the time to clean your child and to gradually show your child how to wash their bodies thoroughly and independently. However, the attitude in which you perform this daily task can convey the value you place on the child himself (i.e. is bath time an interruption to your plans or is it a fun together time?) and you can use the time spent in the bath to sing virtue songs or rhymes.

Character training can occur as you work around the home, as you interact with your child, and as you are out and about – every moment of every day is an opportunity to train. I find this so exciting as it gives enormous value to the seemingly mundane and neutral tasks and activities of my parenting day.

For example, I can view the 700 odd lunches I make for my toddler as a repetitive necessity for nutrition only, or I can see it as an opportunity to train in patience, thankfulness and the beginnings of table etiquette.

Likewise, the myriad of tasks parents of toddlers need to repeat daily can be seen either as chores, or as opportunities to train. Can you see how each part of your day can be used to display or teach a character virtue?

As a parent of a toddler you may have one small time each day where you will specifically sit down for just a few minutes and focus on teaching a character virtue through a story, song or toy.

However, most of your character training can occur through the standard activities of your day. The following chapters will give you a few ideas of how to use everyday activities as training tools. However, I'm sure you will be able to extend and adapt these few ideas to your personal situation.

School Years

During these years, you are imposing a structure of a daily pattern that reflects your own faith and life goals. The implementation of a pattern of daily chores shows that you value everyone's contribution to the family team. The emphasis on sport or music or academics or drama or creative arts or other hobbies shows the value of these in your world view. The regular, semi-regular or occasional attendance at church speaks loudly to the esteem in which you hold that practice. Your allocation of energy, time and money clearly shows your child what you most treasure.

Teen Years

The teens I teach, and those I observe in other settings, are characterised by three things, they are worshippers, consumers and they feel entitled. They all worship something. It may be pleasure, comfort, music, famous individuals, sports, wealth, health, success, self or God. It is clearly seen in their daily attitudes, priorities and discussions. Teens rapidly consume the latest information, music, entertainment, adrenaline experience, concert, event, fashion and holidays. They are constantly in pursuit of the next fun thing. It is clearly seen in their spending, their time and their words. Most, although not all, teens feel that they deserve to do well without effort, to land the first job they apply for, to have the relationship they choose and so on. They feel like they are here to be served. It is clearly seen in their actions, attitudes and words.

Your attitudes and actions in your daily life will model to your teen what you truly worship, desire to consume and how you view your position in the world. The idol of your heart will be revealed through the focus of your energy, time and resources. Model carefully and well.

Deuteronomy 6:6-7 'These commandments that I give you today are to be upon your hearts. Impress them on your children, talk about them when you sit at home and when you walk along the road, when you lie down and when you get up.'

17

Self-Control

Self – a person's or thing's own individuality or essence; composed of one's own personality, affairs, emotions, behaviour and character.

Control – direct; subject to guidance; in proper order; hold in check; regulate, verify.

One of the most beautiful presents you can give your toddler is the virtue of self-control. To gift your child with the ability to manage their own emotions, words and behaviour is truly precious, and will benefit them throughout every facet of their life.

Patiently guiding your toddler towards obtaining self-control takes a lot of dedication and love. It requires time, lots of time, every day. It can be primarily taught through play in a positive, encouraging manner, and so may be enjoyable and fun for both the parent and toddler.

I have already given many examples of activities you can use as tools to train self-control into your toddler's day. Self-control does not simply appear one day. Rather, it is accumulating little by little, day after day, within the framework of an orderly environment.

It is unfair for a parent to expect a child to show self-control if the child has not first been instructed, encouraged and taught how to show self-control in various situations. Too many parents try to correct or modify behaviours without first taking the time to positively train their child, over and over, in that particular area.

Self-control is the base virtue on which all the other virtues rely. In other words, self-control goes hand in hand with every other virtue. It takes a lot of self-control to show kindness, patience, obedience, gentleness and every other virtue.

For example, self-control will enable a child to obey – doing what he knows he should do even though he may not feel like doing it. Or a child may want to hit out at her brother for breaking a toy, but will have the self-control to take the toy to mum for help instead.

Self-control will enable a toddler, who doesn't really enjoy her vegetables, to eat them anyway because dad has said to do so. Self-control will enable your little one to play quietly while you chat uninterrupted on the phone.

Self-control will also help your toddler stay in her big bed, even though there is no physical barrier keeping her there. Self-control will enable your toddler to say, 'I'm sad' or 'I'm angry' rather than scream, kick or sob uncontrollably.

The examples above are not an idealistic dream. Many parents who have diligently trained their child daily in self-control are regularly experiencing these behaviours. These parents are greatly enjoying these toddler years and the fruits of their gentle training, and love spending time with their child each day.

Toddlers characterised by self-control are very contented children. They have learned to be patient and show kindness to those around them and can greatly enjoy their toys because they sit and play for extended periods of time. A child who is cheerfully guided from one fun activity to the next each day, is far happier than one who is left to make their own choices during the day and who is prone to frequent tantrums.

Every activity within your flexible day can be used to train your toddler in self-control. Do remember to add more pre-school type activities into your day as your child moves towards three years of age and beyond. Examples include pre-school activity books, more advanced craft projects, cutting and pasting skills and number recognition lessons. Other examples are simple board games, card games, Bible and general knowledge activities, and more outside activities such as mini-golf, croquet, quoits, hopscotch, T-ball, a mini basketball hoop, trampoline, scooters and skates.

Also, do keep extending the time your child spends on each activity (known as task persistence). A fifteen-month-old may be interested in Playdoh, for example, for five minutes. But with an encouraging voice you can extend that by a few minutes each week, so by the time she is two-years-old, she can play for thirty minutes. Not only does mum get thirty minutes to herself but, more importantly, the toddler is learning the self-control of sitting and focusing which is so essential for future academic learning and all other virtues.

School Years

At school your child will need self-control to line up, to sit still on the mat, to follow instructions, to take turns, to put their hand up and wait for the teacher to help them, to accept not being chosen for a game, to wait until break time to eat, to complete the task they are given, to listen quietly in assembly, to walk and not run down the stairs, to read the library books carefully, to wear the correct uniform and for many other parts of the school day. Having a flexible pattern before and after school each weekday that includes a balance of play, chores, homework and family fun is the best foundation on which self-control training can continue through these years.

Teen Years

In high school, self-control will be needed to get that assignment in on time, to study for exams, to complete all set exercises, to read the assigned novel, to participate in the science experiment or sport class even if it isn't their favourite thing to do, to present a report in front of the class, to hold back a snide remark to a teasing comment by a classmate, to respectfully appeal a teacher's decision, to come last without wallowing in self-pity and to come first without boasting, to sit with quiet reverence through a sombre assembly and to participate to the best of their ability for their sporting team on carnival days.

In other areas of their life teens will need self-control to be on time for their part-time job, to obey instructions from their supervisor and to work diligently until the end of their shift. They will need self-control to treat their romantic partner with kindness, respect and purity. They will need self-control to make decisions regarding music, fashion, alcohol, drugs, smoking, entertainment and social media. Your work in those early years has the potential to bear much fruit in each of these areas.

Titus 2:12 'To live lives that are self-controlled, upright and godly.'

> *We have loved buying, passing on and recommending Mel's books to others.*
>
> *We didn't come to use Growing Families materials until ours were 8, 10 and 12. We first read Terrific Toddlers and facilitated the toddler course when ours were all teenagers. We both cried because we could see with hindsight the value of careful, intentional training in the toddler years and were reaping some of the 'harvest' of not doing this.*
>
> *However, we persevered in working together on our parenting, being intentional in the years that we did have. Loving when we KNEW it didn't feel like it was deserved. Praying like anything, when times looked hopeless. God graciously brought our three children into a living faith in His Son and has blessed them each with spouses with whom we believe they are equally yoked.*
>
> **Jennie, Mum to 3, and Grandmother**

18

Obedience

Obedience – in accordance with; submission to rule; compliance to authority or command.

As parents, we are an authority over our children. We determine what and when they eat (nutrition), when and where they play (safety), what sports they will initially pursue (physical) and what they wear each day according to the weather (health). We also decide what they play with and learn (educational), whom they mix with (social) and we also determine what values and beliefs they will be taught (spiritual).

Establishing our parental authority also involves training our children to obey us. Basically, it will require abundant praise for compliance and a firm consequence for noncompliance.

This training is progressive.

You cannot expect obedience without first instructing your child in how to obey. This can, and should, be achieved in a gentle and loving manner. Once you have basic obedience, then your efforts to train in all the other virtues will be greatly enhanced.

The *Growing Families Australia* parenting courses and books provide excellent information on why obedience is such a vital part of parenting. Details of the courses can be obtained from their website (the address is on the last page).

Training to obedience will unavoidably involve some conflict because our children desire to be self-governing and self-pleasing. You can choose to gently establish your authority and start working towards obedience from when your child is approximately one year of age, before major areas of conflict arise. At this age, this process can be overwhelmingly positive, proactive and characterised by much praise.

Or, you can choose to begin to establish your authority from when your child is around two years of age, and is well and truly into the pattern of exerting his self-will. This process will be mostly reactive and negative and characterised by firm consequences.

Do not lose heart if you are beginning to guide your two or three-year-old toward obedience. It is challenging work, but much easier to do now than one or two more years down the track.

The key to training your child to a standard of obedience is consistency. If you ask for obedience and follow through some of the time and other times you don't, you will experience very little success. You must be consistent.

The parent must be prepared to follow through with a consequence if the child chooses not to obey. If you are not able to follow through, then do not give an instruction in the first place. Ask yourself 'Do I have the time right now to deal with a 'No' response?' If you don't, then avoid giving an instruction. For example, if dinner is on the table and ready to be served, I would simply pick up my young toddler and pop them in the highchair, rather than request that they come.

To start training toward obedience you may choose to use the following suggestions.

At first, be close to your child, not on the other side of the room (too many distractions) and simply call his name. When he has come to you, and you have full eye contact, give a very short instruction. Use a firm, quiet voice and expect him to say 'Yes, mum' and obey.

Give verbal praise, 'What a good boy for obeying mummy!' (or similar) and a big hug. If he chooses not to obey then maybe say 'Oh no, that's a bad choice' (or similar) and walk your child through the required response with lots of verbal praise and affirmation. As much as you can during these early training days try to base your instructions around activities your toddler enjoys. This may include things like morning tea, brushing their teeth, or toy play. Try to have the same few instructions at similar times each day to aid the learning process.

You may choose to repeat this process only a few times during your day, at times when your toddler is fairly content. I found my toddlers were much more responsive to this training in the morning, rather than the late afternoon. By limiting the number of times you are expecting obedience during this initial stage, you should experience a high success rate. It also helps mum and dad to be consistent.

After you have consistently walked your child through this process for a short time, maybe a few days or a week, you can then calmly apply a firm, immediate negative consequence for non-compliance. We reserved our strongest consequences for disobedience and safety issues only. This ensured they were effective as they were rare and certainly stood out. Overuse of any one method of correction will be ineffective, so do ensure you use a variety of positive and negative consequences. For all other behaviour issues, we used logical consequences.

When you have established the pattern of obedience at these few times during the day, then you can gradually increase the number of times you expect obedience in your toddler's day. Your toddler will not be obedient in all situations within a few weeks. You will need to first train them to be obedient at home, then even when they are tired at home or when visitors are in the home. Then you will gently train toward expecting obedience when you are out in a public place. Then, train your toddler to obey even when every other child is doing the wrong thing. Finally, train to obedience in situations where you ask them to do something they would possibly prefer not to do!

So how do you respond to your child's behaviour for the rest of the day during this training stage? Firstly, one option is to simply take your child to where they need to be, rather than asking for obedience. For example, if it is time for a bath, pick your child up and pop her in the bath. If it is time for dinner, take her hand

and walk her to the table. If you want the toys packed up, then make it a fun game with mum (probably) doing most of the work.

This greatly reduces the frustration level for mum and child. Over the next few weeks, as your child begins to be characterised by obedience, you can say 'Please hop in your bath', 'Please come to dinner' and 'Please pack up your toys' and she will!

Secondly, another option is to use logical consequences. I also call these positive consequences because they are an effective way of managing behaviour without nagging, yelling or smacking.

If your home is characterised by an atmosphere of praise and happy encouragement then you will find these suggestions very effective. In an orderly and calm environment, you will have far fewer behavioural problems than if your toddler was meandering from toy to toy, or TV show to TV show, or from inside to outside on their own whim. Simply by having a routine, you are covertly, but powerfully, showing your authority, in that it is mum and dad who plan the day, not toddler.

Over the page are a few examples of logical consequences that may be suitable for your toddler. I want to emphasise that these personal examples are suggestions only. You may implement others that are more relevant or practical for you.

Issue	Logical Consequence
Talking or singing loudly in the morning before wake-up time	Simply stays in cot until alarm goes off
Chooses not to eat lunch	No food until dinner
Throws all toys out of playpen	Stay in playpen for usual time anyway
Chooses not to sit to watch Playschool on TV	Sit in cot until Playschool is finished
Repeatedly touch mum's craft magazines or make-up	Remove the object or the child.
Fussing or whining about having to play outside alone	Plays outside anyway, fuss or no fuss
Chooses not to play with toys on highchair	Child just sits in highchair
Two siblings fighting over one truck	Remove that truck for a few days
Chooses to respond with a 'No' to an instruction	Isolate to the cot for five to fifteen minutes
Throws book on floor during reading time	Sits with no book for rest of reading time
Chooses not to sleep for the afternoon nap	Stays in cot
Chooses not to sit on a small chair for afternoon tea and video	Pop in highchair to watch and eat
Scream for bath wash	Wash anyway
Child is a little grizzly after waking up from a nap	A few minutes of cuddles is often helpful
Plays with toys rather than reading just before bed	Light goes off
Calls out after lights out for night sleep	No parental response is given (Nappy, warmth, and thirst checked first of course)

Mum is speaking quietly and calmly throughout each of these situations and is very much in control, without any nagging and not one smack.

Two things to note.

First, you cannot expect behaviours that you have not diligently trained your child in first.

For example, it is unfair to suddenly expect your little one to sit for thirty minutes to watch a video – you need to gradually build up to that time, maybe starting with just five minutes the first week.

Or, you cannot expect your toddler to accept the food you offer for lunch, if sometimes you provide something else in response to their whining, and other times you don't. Consistent expectations and responses are crucial for effective training.

Or, for example, it would be unfair to expect your toddler to play outside for thirty minutes all by himself without first showing him the types of play he can enjoy outside. You will need to spend time showing him all the things he can do with the sand toys or the bats and balls, or even how to ride his tricycle.

Nor can you expect a 'No' to be obeyed if the 'No' sometimes means 'No', sometimes means 'Later', and at other times, actually means, 'Yes'. You must be consistent and truthful in your instructions.

Nor can you expect siblings to share toys nicely if you have not spent time (hours and hours over many, many days) patiently teaching them how to share and how to come to mum for help when needed.

Secondly, once you have a basic standard of obedience in your toddler's day established, you may choose to make one or two issues at a time the focus of your training.

For example, whereas previously you isolated for not sitting still to watch a TV program, you may now make it a direct obedience issue by requesting, 'Sit here to watch'. Disobedience will be met with a calm but firm and immediate consequence. Once that behaviour is generally established, then you can move onto another behaviour.

Dealing with one issue at a time is manageable for mum and dad and it enables the day to still be mostly positive. It also helps the improvements to be clearly visible.

If you are trying to work on ten issues at a time, you will see little fruit and probably feel quite discouraged. Working with one issue at a time is fairer also to the child, as it does not overwhelm him with a myriad of expectations on one day.

Are you not comfortable with the idea of gently and patiently training toward obedience?

Someone will have authority in your home.

Will it be the parent or the toddler who determines the menu, the general atmosphere in the home, the activities of the family, the quality and frequency of social interactions, the amount of time mum and dad will have to themselves, the daily routine, the shopping experience, and so on?

Who will rule whom?

School Years

It is not always wise to obey. Sadly, we need to instruct our children on when it is not okay to obey an adult. You do not need to go into the details of why an adult is not safe, but you do need to teach them how to respond in those situations.

I gave my school aged children a password and they could only ever go home with another adult after school in my absence if that adult told them the password. If not, they were to run to the nearest teacher or the office. If any adult or older child, even if it was someone they knew very well, made them feel 'Icky in their tummy', through their words or actions, they could say a loud 'No thanks' and come straight to me.

Teen Years

Your teens will be asked to do things by other teens or adults that make them feel uncomfortable. Talking through as many of these potential scenarios beforehand is most helpful. My teens knew they could always offer the 'I would need to talk to my parents about that first' as an easy way out of a pressure situation. Also, letting them know that they can ring you at any time and you will pick them up is a handy back-up to organise in advance.

Proverbs 29:15 'A child left to his own way, disgraces his mother.'

> *I am inspired by Mel's honesty, consistency, and love for her Lord and her children. Mel has provided a host of practical examples and applications. These examples are worked off principles that can be applied across the spectrum from toddlers to teens. I find that I believe I can make positive changes because her words are inspirational and her suggestions are attainable.*
>
> **Heather, Mum to 7**

> *One of many things I am thankful my parents taught me, was how to be different from other girls. How to show Jesus, not my legs, how to speak kindly and demonstrate maturity. They taught me that everything I do and say matters, I may not think one little slip up is a big deal, but there is always someone looking up to me. There may be reasons for saying or doing certain things, but they are no excuse. I am now 18 and truly grateful for these values and high standards.*
>
> **Izzy, age 18**

19

Speech

Speech – use articulate utterance in ordinary voice; make known one's opinion, the truth etc.

A toddler who is characterised by pleasant words is a joy to have around. Unfortunately, teaching a toddler to control his tongue is one of the most overlooked areas of training. Don't waste these daily opportunities to work on a little more self-control training. It is very possible to teach a small child to manage the volume, content and quantity of his speech.

In this area, more so than many others, the parental example is key. My dear friend, Jo, always endeavours to speak very politely and quietly to her four children. All of her children are a delight to be around as they are so polite and well-spoken, and in no way overbearing. They are extremely happy and content, too. She is a huge example to me of loving parenting.

Volume – Children will naturally raise their voices when angry, hurt, frustrated, excited, surprised, happy and during the course of general play. This is all very normal and simply a part of childhood, and most appropriate at times. We are not trying to stop all loud noise.

However, as parents, we can certainly help our children modify the excessively loud noises. Prolonged screeching and screaming at a very high pitch is not very appropriate in most situations, nor is it considerate of others who may be around.

Do model a quiet voice (a whisper) an inside voice (normal talking voice) and an outside voice (a little louder but not at the top of the lungs) in the appropriate situations. Explain when and why you might use each one, for example, 'Let's use our whisper voice when we visit Uncle today as he is not very well'.

You can play a fun game with your toddler to demonstrate when to use which voice. For example, ask the trucks (or bears or dolls) to speak in a whisper voice while at the truck doctor's surgery (we don't want to hurt the ears of the sick trucks). Or have the truck use a loud and happy, but not screaming, voice when the other truck gives one truck a surprise present.

Give lots of praise for using the appropriate volume, and patient and gentle verbal reminders when they don't. If my toddler would get a little too loud during outside play, I usually found that a pleasant word ('Oops, I think Mr. Bear might be waking up with that loud noise') would help tone her down again. If you diligently work on this, little by little, you will see improvement.

Content – Be very clear about what words you will allow to be spoken in your home. Also, be clear about what words you will not allow to be spoken in your home. For example, 'I hate you', 'I wish you would go away', 'You are ugly', or 'You are a horrible parent', were not permitted in our home.

We are not suppressing the emotions our toddler experiences. Rather we are gradually training them to express the emotions appropriately. Always give your child an alternative phrase to use to replace the one you are correcting. For example, 'I hate you', in response to a sibling snatching a toy can be modified to 'I feel sad that you took my toy'. Be sure to give lots of praise and a big hug when you hear the new phrases.

Teach your child about the power of words through verses, songs and role-plays. Read books about children who speak kind words and discuss how our words make the other person feel. Make up stories that feature your child in familiar situations saying kind words, or dealing with her emotions in the right way. Make your story into a book and include photos of your child. Your toddler will love it, and will be learning for future situations too.

One of my children, during his pre-toddler and then toddler years, gradually moved from squealing when a sibling snatched a toy to firmly stating 'I feel sad', as he stomped off to his bed to calm down (on his own initiative). Finally he moved to 'Let's take turns'. It is so rewarding watching this transition, and it makes the hundreds of times you instruct in this all worthwhile in the end.

Quantity – Many toddlers seem to be able to speak non-stop from morning to night. This chatter is often delightful and it is such a joy to experience the developing vocabulary during this toddler stage. Sometimes it seems the child is articulating every single thought that passes through the mind.

If, however, your toddler is characterised by talking all the time with barely a minute's break during the day, and by asking question after question, then you probably have an opportunity to train your child in verbal self-control. Even if the comments and questions are positive or neutral in themselves, the constant stream of words needs to be addressed.

Do ensure you are having a special one-to-one time each day with your verbal toddler. I tried to give Emily fifteen or twenty minutes of my undivided attention with full eye contact, early on in each day. This enabled her to share many of the important things on her mind and helped her to feel loved and heard. It did seem to cut down a little of the chatter during the rest of the day too.

By kneeling down to eye level and giving her my full attention when she spoke to me during the day, she cut down the many repeats, as I had heard and responded the first time. I would also gently instruct her to get my attention first, by placing her hand on me, and waiting (with lips closed) until I was smiling and looking right at her eyes before she began to talk. This behaviour was greatly reinforced with a cuddle and an abundance of praise.

Emily's day, when she was a toddler, was divided into mostly thirty or sixty minute segments. During this time, I gave very clear instructions as to which activities were talking ones and which were not.

For example, during room time, reading time and outside play I encouraged her not to talk to mummy. A stream of words to her imaginary friends characterised her outside playtime. This was very cute to listen to, especially as I didn't have to try and keep up with the rapid changes in topics and provide answers.

The mealtime, craft time, focus play, family time and most other times were talking times. I was in no way trying to suppress all her talking; rather I was aiming to gently teach her that there are times to talk and times to be quiet.

If your verbal toddler is overly dominant in social situations, then give very clear concrete instructions about what she should say just before the guests arrive. 'Please don't talk too much', is meaningless to your toddler. How can they determine what 'too much' is?

Rather you may choose to instruct her to share two bits of news (be specific) with Mrs Smith, and then play with the toys. Also, even your two-year old can be pre-armed with a question (just one or two) to ask Mrs Smith, so that the conversation is not one-sided.

Do not expect your toddler to succeed in this immediately. It is a process that takes a lot of patient instruction. Role-play manners and teach conversation skills for social situations during your playtimes at home, with tea sets and dolls and bears as guests.

Always give the reasons why we take turns to talk (be kind to others, show respect for elders, and so on), and have your toddler give you the reasons behind verbal manners. If she says it herself, then she is more likely to remember it, and then, eventually do it too!

School Years

When I am on playground duty at school, I have a stream of students approaching me with reports of what other children have said to them. I listen, ask them how they feel about that, then I ask them to think of something extraordinarily kind they can say back to that student. They look at me stunned. That was not the response they were expecting. Speaking words that are characterised by self-control, wisdom and kindness brings peace.

Teen Years

I have met many fantastic teens in my travels speaking around Australia. One of their outstanding features is their speech. They speak quietly indoors, and appropriately outside. They speak words of fun and encouragement to their siblings. They show respect to their parents and are able and willing to converse with me, their visitor. They listen well and ask good questions. They are cheerful, positive and friendly. Their parents have obviously trained them well in the area of speech and they are reaping the beautiful fruit of this.

Proverbs 25:11 'A word fitly spoken is like apples of gold in a setting of silver.'

As a teen, respect is something I value and I am very grateful that my parents raised me to be respectful to those around me. When I was around the age of 14, I asked my parents why I had to say Mrs Foote or Mrs Hayde and they told me it was the respectful thing to do. I didn't quite understand their answer for a while, but then I saw the way it helped me at school. It is because I respect others and treat them the way I was raised to, I have noticed that people are willing to help me when I need it.

Respect is the reason I have the amazing friends and family supporting my walk with Christ. The way my parents encouraged me to spend time with Christ and to help others was a vital part of my upbringing, the way they respected me helped me to respect them as parents and as the most important people in my life.

Stephanie, age 17

20

Kindness

Kindness – gentle or benevolent nature; friendly in one's conduct to; affectionate.

Kindness is a very abstract virtue. It is quite difficult to verbally explain it to a toddler.

However, this does not mean we can't teach our toddler to be kind. We simply need to demonstrate kindness in a concrete way by modelling kindness through everyday situations.

I greatly enjoy teaching kindness to my children, as it is very positive training and lots of fun. The look of pure delight on their faces when they know they have chosen to be kind is priceless. It is such a joy to hear them running in saying 'Mummy, mummy I was kind to Katie when . . .' The pride they show in their right choice is gorgeous.

The basis of kindness is thinking of the other person, not self. Our toddlers will naturally think firstly of themselves, and so we will need to be proactive and persistent in patiently teaching our child to think of others too.

A key part of teaching kindness during the toddler years is to emphasize to your child how other people feel. Use very simple words to describe the emotions, such as 'sad' and 'happy' during this initial training, and use similar phrases each time to reinforce the learning.

For example, you may say, 'Katie was very sad when you . . .', or 'Well done, Katie felt very happy when you . . .' A toddler is still very egocentric and so you need to constantly draw their attention to how their behaviour and choices will be affecting those around them.

When your toddler is familiar with the idea of others feeling 'happy' or 'sad' you can role-play various scenarios (with bears, dolls or trucks) and have your child tell you (not you tell your child) how the bear, doll or truck would feel. Keep these role-plays very short (less than a minute or two) and fun. Your toddler will love giving you the right answer.

Kindness training is not another thing to add to your day. You can use everyday activities to verbally explain, and then physically demonstrate, exactly what kindness will look like in a particular situation. It is important to use a happy, patient voice during your instructions.

Also, do try to be proactive, rather than reactive, in your parenting. For example, to be proactive, you could sit with your children as they share a new toy; explaining and demonstrating how to kindly take turns. This is fun and positive for both the children and parent.

Or you could be reactive by giving them the new toy without any demonstration or supervision, and only interrupt when they are in the middle of squabbling over the new toy. This is unpleasant and negative for both the children and the parent.

Below are examples of a few everyday situations you can use as opportunities to teach kindness. Don't lecture, just happily explain and quickly demonstrate once, and then move on to the next part of your day. Your toddler will slowly catch on over the next months, if you are calm and patient.

Buy a treat while shopping and have your toddler kindly share it with rest of family when she gets home.

Praise her for being kind and, after a time, maybe a very long time, she will initiate the thinking of others herself.

Swing on the swings for ten pushes (the concept of 'time' is too abstract for a toddler) and then let's be kind and let your sister have a turn on the swing for ten pushes.

Put your clothes in the basket just before hopping into the bath to be kind to the next person who wants to use the bathroom.

Show kindness to Thomas by choosing some toys to bring out that you think Thomas might like to play with when he comes over soon.

All chores that you do with your toddler's 'help' can be used to talk about how we are showing kindness to our visitors and family members.

Pick a flower, or make up a posy, for friends you are about to visit.

Draw a picture to say thank you for a present, gifts of second-hand clothes or toys, or a lovely visit. Later you can have your pre-school child write their name on the bottom of a picture they draw, and then later still, when they are school age, they can write their own thank you notes. This is a basic kindness that is sadly lacking in society today.

Be kind to others and tidy up these blocks so that no one can trip or stub their toe.

Play quietly in this room while baby has a sleep. This is kind as it allows baby to get the rest he needs to grow big and strong.

I'm sure you will have many, many other moments in your day where you can patiently demonstrate kindness to your toddler.

Enjoy building this virtue into your child's heart.

School Years

Encourage your child to think of others during the school years. Maybe pop an extra muffin in their lunch box and have them choose a friend to give it to at lunch time. Have them invite a friend over to play who often doesn't get asked on a playdate. Ensure that you ask all the class (or just all the girls or just all the boys) to your child's party, as leaving one or two out is unkind. At dinner each night, ask them if they had an opportunity to show kindness to anyone that day to model the importance of this practice.

Teen Years

Provide regular ways for your teen to show kindness to his family. For example, one could be in charge of creating a Saturday morning café style breakfast for the family. Or one teen could be in charge of keeping mum's car washed, vacuumed and filled with oil and water as a practical act of kindness. Or a teen could have a regular weekly time where he plays games of the younger sibling's choosing. Thank them for showing kindness in this way.

Ephesians 4:32 'Be kind to one another, tender hearted.'

> *Amongst many things that my parents taught me as a child there is one thing I appreciate the most. I am by far not a perfect child, not a goody two shoes or quiet sit still kind of girl. I was antsy, disobedient, rebellious, and the one who wanted to push the boundaries as hard and far as I could. Yet Mum and Dad had a tight routine (implementing the funnel) for me not allowing me to get away with anything and disciplining me when I did do something naughty. In the long run, it has helped me to respect others particularly those in authority.*
>
> **Josie, age 17**

21

Patience

Patience – calm endurance of provocation; forbearance; quiet and self-possessed waiting.

I used to think I was a fairly patient person, this was before I had children.

Over the first ten years of my parenting journey I focused, from time to time, on teaching my children to be patient. Inadvertently I discovered that I too had grown greatly in my ability to be patient in most situations. Who has been trained, I wonder?

Patience may be defined, for a toddler, as waiting with no talking, complaining or movement. This changes the abstract concept of patience into concrete, achievable behaviours.

As with all training, you will instruct, supervise and demonstrate this virtue over many, many days. Teaching is not just telling. You need to instruct clearly and follow this up with many examples that your toddler can see. Then you will need to supervise and help your toddler in an encouraging manner to master the task herself. This may take many days, weeks, or months of repetition.

Toddlers are still very young, so give them time to learn. Be wary of expecting too much too soon. Even many adults struggle to have the self-control to wait patiently in a shop queue or a traffic jam, for example.

Your voice needs to be happy and calm, and you need to shower your child with praise. You will initially expect it only a few times a day, and for very, very small increments of time. You will very gradually provide more situations in which your child can demonstrate patience, and for increasingly longer periods of time.

Let me share just one personal example of patience training. At ten months of age, Caleb would indicate that he wanted his meal as soon as he was in his highchair. So, I would ensure his meal was ready before I placed him in his chair, and fed him straight away. Over the next few months I gently aimed to stretch this time out.

By about twelve months of age he could (sometimes) manage to wait for up to two minutes before he would express his impatience for dinner. By about fifteen months of age he could regularly wait for five minutes in his highchair before the meal was served. So, it took around five months, or approximately 420 meals, of consistent encouragement (never negative) to teach Caleb to wait quietly and still for just five minutes. Was it worth it?

Yes.

By the time he was eighteen months old he had enough self-control to show patience in cafes and restaurants, when I was chatting to a friend on the phone, in doctor waiting rooms, at the bus stop, in supermarket queues and many other everyday situations. He was a pleasure to take out and was constantly praised for his display of quiet patience by shop assistants, waitresses and friends. This was very affirming for him.

By the time he was two years of age Caleb was most capable of waiting for twenty to thirty minutes, if necessary. I would usually provide a book or quiet toy for him during these waiting times if appropriate.

Please note that I did not suddenly expect my two-year-old to wait quietly for ten minutes. I gave many, many instructions and much praise over many months to get to that point. Also, I did not expect Caleb to show patience outside the home without extensive practice in the home first.

Within the framework of an orderly day you will have many snippets of time where you can build a little patience. Be wary of expecting too much too soon, maybe just starting with a minute at a time.

Also, don't get bogged down in this training at any one point in your day. Mention patience very briefly, in just a sentence, and then move on with your day. An upbeat positive tone will be far more effective than a frustrated, negative tone.

Below are a few examples of patience training:

- Please stay at the table while mummy gets the crayons out of the drawer.
- Please wait patiently on the bed while I straighten your room.
- You may eat your dinner while you wait patiently for mum and dad to finish our conversation.
- I need you to read this book patiently while lunch is being made.
- Patiently sit on this mat with your hands on your knees, I'll be with you in just a moment.
- Let's practice counting our fingers (or reciting our ABC) while we patiently wait for our turn at the supermarket checkout.
- You could climb on the bridge over here until the boy finishes his turn on the swing.

Keeping your expectations very small at first will heighten the likelihood of success, as will the very liberal doses of praise give every time.

Simple board games that require waiting for turns are a direct way of teaching patience to your toddler and pre-school child. They are great fun too!

School Years

There is lots of waiting in each school day. Teaching your child patience in those early years will greatly help them cope with the realities of school life. One of the easiest ways to continue to teach patience throughout the school years is to play board games as a family. These naturally involve waiting your turn and you can play longer and more complicated games as they grow in this skill. Teaching them how to wait in the café until their snack or meal is served is also good practice. Do you want to practice conversation skills during this time, or give them a book to read or an activity book to complete while they wait? Waiting with quiet words and a still body takes a great deal of self-control and is a valuable life skill.

Teen Years

I have been teaching teens for many years now. Many are characterised by impatience. They say they can't wait for the new movie or game to be released, and they say they can't wait for that next concert, holiday, party or adventure. They can't wait for the lesson to be over, for the final bell of the day to ring and, most of all, for their time at school to be finally finished. Their impatience for the next thing is robbing them of the joy of the moment. Teaching your teen to be patient for the next season, by appreciating and enjoying the present, is a great gift for them.

Colossians 3:12 'As God's chosen ones, holy and dearly loved, clothe yourselves with compassion, kindness, humility, meekness and patience.'

> *As an adult, I am now thankful that Mum never let me win. NEVER. I was five years old, and I'd just learnt how to play Uno! So, I play a lovely game of Uno with my mum, only to lose again, and again, and again, and . . . you get the idea. I kept trying really hard until, the day finally came when I won. Mum smiled, looked me in the eye and said, 'Well done, you beat me fair and square'. She pointed out to me that I had earned that win, and I finally understood.*
>
> *Mum used this concept in many areas of my life. She was proud of me no matter what, but she wasn't going to shower me in 'false praise'. She never let me believe that near enough was good enough... she always encouraged me to strive for greatness, telling me that I was capable of more. Mum taught me that I have to earn my achievements, and to do this, I have to push myself. This prepared me for adulthood; I have to apply myself to better myself. If I want to win, I have to earn it.*
>
> **Jake, age 19**

22

Friendship

Friendship – characteristic of showing, expressing, or prompted by kindness; on amicable terms with.

Siblings can be best friends.

Many of the young mothers I speak to express the thought that hopefully, somehow, eventually, their children will get on well with each other and not fight all the time. I want to encourage you that this does not have to be simply wishful thinking. As proactive and positive parents, we can purposefully encourage and guide our children, to not only get along well with each other but to develop their relationship into one of being best friends.

Even before the new brother or sister arrives, you can prepare your toddler by referring to the baby-to-be as a special friend. Include your toddler in as many of the preparations as you can and speak happily about all the benefits of having a sibling. We constantly use the word 'friend' when talking to our children about their siblings to create the expectation that they are indeed friends, it is not an option! We tell them that it is very nice to have other friends, and of course they spend time with other children, but these friends may come and go. However, the friends for life will be their siblings.

It was quite amusing, one day, hearing three-year-old Caleb talking to two-year-old Emily about how he would look after her and give her yummy dinners (no vegetables) if mum and dad were not around anymore. He was showing his understanding, at that age, of caring for his sister always. More recently, all three of them have been discussing plans to buy houses in the same street when they are grown-ups so they can still see each other every day.

A flexible pattern for your day will provide the best framework for developing friendships among siblings. Do think through your feeding times for the new baby and make the necessary adjustments to your toddler's day a few months before baby arrives. This will mean that your toddler's day will not change too much when baby actually arrives.

Think through the best times for toddler and baby to spend together each day. You will want to choose times when you are free to supervise and encourage gentle touching. By being proactive here, the interaction will be overwhelmingly positive, and this will greatly enhance your toddler's feelings towards the baby.

Also ensure that the special one-to-one times you have with your toddler now continue after baby arrives. They may be shorter on some days, especially as you adjust initially, but positive time with your toddler will greatly reduce any negative feelings your toddler may experience during this time of change.

As your children grow, organise your day into activities that promote harmony and fun for both children. Do not expect them to naturally be able to be happily together all day every day. Be proactive and make all of the decisions in a matter-of-fact voice that depicts your gentle authority.

Here are a few examples of how you might arrange your day to promote friendship between siblings.

Plan time where the older child can play alone to build his towers or set up her dolls without interruption from the younger one. If the younger child is constantly allowed to disturb the other's play, the older one will become resentful. Plan time for each of them to have special focus time just with mum, every day. They will each feel loved and are less likely to be competing for mum's attention during the rest of the day.

Maybe have the younger one in a highchair, and the older one in a small child's lounge seat so both can watch a short video without interrupting each other. Set both children up on either end of the kitchen bench with their own lump of

Playdoh and own tools so that they can play happily out of reach but side-by-side. Seat one child on each side of you (the same side every time, mum and dad choose this) for story time so there are no squabbles about whose turn it is to sit on mum's knee. It is not fun to deal with the same conflict issue day after day. You can all look forward to story time this way.

Have the same cup, bowl, placemat, chair etc. for each child for each meal (mum and dad choose this) so as to limit any verbal disagreements. Where to sit and eat each meal, and snack time, and what dishes to use, doesn't need to be an everyday source of conflict. Keep things simple for all. Ensure you are very clear about what toys are for general sharing and which toys belong to one person. For example, the sand toys may be for everyone to share but the bikes belong to a particular child. If Sam rides Sam's bike and Emily rides Emily's bike, the daily scramble to get to the best bike first is eliminated.

You may have one child playing in the lounge room for twenty or thirty minutes and the other playing in the family room. This will give each child a chance to play independently, and hopefully, make them more eager to play with each other after a time apart.

By keeping your day ordered and calm, your children will experience mostly positive interactions with each other, and mum or dad are not frantically rushing from conflict to conflict all day. Have fun each day as you constantly instil the virtue of friendship into your everyday activities. Here are a few examples to get you started.

Take your toddler with you to choose a birthday, Christmas or 'any day' gift for their best friend. Have her help you wrap the gift and then draw on the card. Let her choose the place to hide the gift until the giving. Your toddler can help you bake muffins or cookies, or draw a special picture, for their best friend who is napping.

When you pick up a new pack of photos sit down together and comment on how happy the children look and how they are such good friends. Pop them in a scrapbook or album and look over them often. Maybe have an inexpensive small book for photos that each child can own.

Teach appropriate touching of hugs and kisses or holding hands. Too much touching may be unpleasant or irritating to one sibling, even if offered in the best intent by another. Maybe you even need to gently teach one child to graciously accept a hug or kiss from a sibling at the appropriate time.

I have really wanted my family to be characterised by hugs with each other, every day, and this continued through the teen years. Create lots of positive memories by enjoying experiences together such as trips to the beach, parks, libraries, museums, shows, visiting friends and supporting each other's interests and hobbies. Cheerfully talk about the memories often, and emphasize the fun siblings can enjoy together.

Teach your toddler simple phrases he can use to show his appreciation for his siblings. Model when and how to use these encouraging words to promote friendship. Show him how to say thank you in response to a compliment. Your toddler is not too young to begin to learn these basic courtesies. In fact, you will probably find him quite responsive.

Now to the bit you are waiting for — teaching siblings to manage conflict situations! These take many forms, but in this book, we will look at just one area — sharing toys.

From my observations, it seems that sibling conflicts usually begin in earnest when the younger child is between twelve and eighteen months of age. One of the major sources of conflict at this early stage seems to be over the sharing (or not sharing!) of toys. Emily was almost eighteen months old and Caleb was three years old when we really focused on teaching them to manage conflict situations.

During this training stage, which lasted about six months, I organised the day so that they only had two thirty minute periods where they actually played together. For the rest of the day they played in different parts of the house or were involved in side-by-side activities that were closely supervised. This helped the training time to be as positive as possible, as conflict was limited to just two spots in the day.

At the start of the first playtime, I would spend maybe three to five minutes sitting with Caleb and Emily and just one toy. I would talk through taking turns with the toy and allow Emily to play with it for half a minute, and then help her give Caleb a turn. I used a fun, encouraging voice and kept this daily positive teaching time very short.

I then let them play together while hovering out of sight. I didn't plan any important task for myself during this time so I wouldn't feel frustrated or interrupted if the children needed my guidance. Inevitably, within a few minutes, Caleb and Emily would be after the same toy. I would quickly go over and cheerfully talk it through. I would ask, 'What do you think you could do now?' and they would both look at me with blank stares. So, I would cheerfully suggest to them 'Let's take turns!' and help them share the toy.

This scenario would be repeated every few minutes or so during that play time and I would (outwardly!) calmly talk them through the situation each time. I would try and end the playtime on a happy note, if possible, not in the middle of a conflict situation. After repeating this many, many times (it felt like a thousand times to me) I was delighted to finally get a 'We could take turns'. Over the next few months, they were gradually able to manage more and more of these situations themselves. At around the sixth month I finally had one playtime all to myself uninterrupted.

As they were able to manage these two play times together I gradually increased the number of times they played together each day. I also continued to provide new situations in which they could learn to share.

For example, whereas previously they had their own colouring book, and their own set of colouring pencils, I would now set them up with their own colouring book, but only one set of coloured pencils to practice taking turns with the colours. Or rather than set them up at each end of the table with their own Playdoh and Playdoh tools, I'd place them close together with one group of tools to use.

Of course, we had some good days and bad days during this whole process. There were a few weeks where I felt they were getting worse at sharing, not better.

Some days, one child was simply not willing to take turns. In this case, I would simply remove the child, or the toy.

Does this sound like a lot of hard work? It certainly felt like it at the time, and I did despair on the odd occasion wondering if they would ever learn to take turns. Working on this issue, and then other issues between them during the toddler years, has reaped such a beautiful friendship between all three of our children. This has bought harmony and enjoyment to the whole family and weekend get-togethers and holidays are eagerly anticipated, not dreaded.

Toddlers can learn to play nicely with their siblings. Your patient perseverance in this teaching will greatly enhance the sibling friendships. They will always have the odd disagreement, that is very normal, but your day does not need to be filled with crying and constant arguments. Please note that this is just my own personal way of teaching toddlers to share. I hope it is a helpful example to you and will stimulate your own ideas on how to positively enhance the relationships between your own little ones.

Of course, as the children mature, we want to move them beyond simply taking turns with their toys. It is truly beautiful when they get to the point of asking their brother or sister if they would like the toy first. This is putting the other person's desires before their own – showing love.

School Years

Sibling friendships were still a focus during the school years. They needed to attend their sibling's soccer finals and ballet concerts (not every game or lesson). They were encouraged to make a card for their sibling's birthday. I took them each shopping for gifts for special occasions which they wrapped, hid and then presented on the day. They had playdates with friends once a week and the other four afternoons were home days. We had family days out or at home with friends two or three times a week in the school holidays, and the other days were siblings only days at home or out. Keep cultivating these relationships and the friendship will keep developing.

Teen Years

Having a backyard pool, an outdoor basketball ring, a table-tennis table, many board games and lots of sporting equipment ensured that we had a houseful of teens on many occasions. Gatherings for key sporting events, How-to-Host-a-Murder dress-up nights, BBQs and games evenings were memorable moments for our teens. Sharing their friends with each other created noise and mess and lots of laughs. Being involved in the same youth group at church also encouraged them to spend lots of time together. As older teens, it was fun to plan adventure type day outings and holidays that further strengthened these bonds of friendship.

1 Peter 3:8 'Live in harmony with one another, be sympathetic, love as brothers, be compassionate and humble.'

> *What comes to mind is the way my parents have always modelled to my siblings and I how we should live and not just told us.*
>
> *Firstly, my Dad has always tried to live as Ephesians 5:25 says in living as a man who is willing to love his wife as 'Christ loved the church, and gave himself up for her'. I see this most clearly in the way my dad seeks to put my mum, and by extension us kids, first.*
>
> *This is emulated through the way he will always help us out if we have an issue, typically of the practical sense, no matter how much sleep he has to lose or how far it puts him behind at work.*
>
> *As for my mum, she has always made time for us, and been the stable rock in my life, second to Jesus! I know that if I have any problem, more typically of the emotional sense, my mum will be there to talk me through it and point me back to Jesus. But this has only come because during my teen years she would rearrange her schedule in order to be around and available when my siblings and I were around.*

Ultimately, my parents have tried to faithfully point me back to Jesus in all that they do, and taught me that seeking Him is all I need in this life. As a young adult, I now realise that these seemingly small acts, day in and day out, that my parents were committed to, have taught me how to approach life with lenses that look for God in all things.

Corinne, age 22

23

Helpfulness

Helpfulness – provide with means towards what is needed or sought; be of service to.

Wouldn't it be great to have a school aged child who could make his own bed, tidy his bedroom, quickly get himself dressed for school, and make his own lunch all before breakfast? Wouldn't it be nice to have him come home, put his bag away, make and clean up his own afternoon tea, and complete family chores without arguing or complaining? Would you like him to do all this without being reminded or nagged?

Not only is this enjoyable for mum, it is incredibly rewarding and satisfying for the child himself. He can be very proud of his initiative and cheerful independence. It also frees up the interaction between parent and child to be positive and relationship focused, rather than negatively focused on behaviour.

One aspect of our parenting task is to teach our children to become progressively more independent and to eventually be able to competently manage all household tasks and personal affairs. Menu planning, budgeting, ironing, washing, minor repairs, dusting, basic sewing skills, scrubbing, maintenance of appliances, nutrition, personal hygiene, baking and cooking are only a few.

I found that focusing on the long-term goals for my child helped with the day-to-day parenting of my toddler. This is particularly true in training your child to be helpful.

For example, Samuel started to help me sweep up the sand and put the sandpit toys away from around eighteen months old. Rather than viewing Samuel's efforts at sweeping as a hindrance (that made the job take twice as long as if I simply did it myself) I could view each day as a step closer to the time when he would manage to do it himself. This kept me motivated and determined to consistently train in this skill, despite the weekly ups and downs of progress or lack thereof. By the time he was four years old he could do a fairly adequate job.

Of course, this meant that I no longer had to tidy the sandpit, which was nice. However, the important part of this training was that Samuel was learning to be helpful. I showered him with praise throughout this training, even in the early days when I did 99% of the sweeping up. He was also learning the virtues of obedience, self-control and perseverance during this process. Later, he tidied the sandpit up without a second thought, it was simply an expected part of his day.

By giving your toddler just one or two very simple chores to do each day, you are providing a foundation on which to build more complex chores later on. For example, your two-year-old can help you make a salad by tearing the lettuce, sprinkling on the cheese or washing the carrots. By the time she is five she may be able to manage the preparation of the whole salad (with your supervision of course).

As your child masters the small tasks you can then allow them to do the bigger tasks. Caleb, at nine years of age, was very excited to finally be big enough to use the whipper snipper for the edges of the grass.

As teens, they each had a night to cook dinner for the family and they looked forward to this. Of course, they loved to choose the dessert but they also genuinely enjoyed this part of their week.

Each family will need to determine for themselves how many general chores they will expect each child to have at which ages. During the toddler years, we personally limited the general chores to one or two tasks each day. This was because we were focusing mainly on helping our toddler learn to manage their own personal responsibilities (e.g. brushing teeth and hair, getting dressed, making the bed, putting own clothes in drawers nicely etc.) during this stage of their development.

For my school aged children, I usually aimed to teach a new chore or recipe or household skill in each school holiday. This kept me focused on moving them towards their independence. They did have the odd grumble now and then, as we all do, but overwhelmingly they accepted the fact that they were an important part of the family and had their jobs to do.

To train your child in helpfulness you will need to clearly instruct many times. Then you will need to demonstrate the task by actually doing it yourself. Then you will supervise her as she does it all by herself. Finally, she will be able to apply your instructions without any help at all.

This sounds very obvious, I know, but it is important to allow time for each of these stages when teaching your child a new task. I would often feel quite frustrated at my child for not performing a task properly and then realise that this was my fault for not instructing or demonstrating adequately first.

I was also surprised at how many times I would need to supervise a task before my child could perform it unsupervised. Emily, for example, was quite willing and able to fold the washing but it took many, many months before she could diligently fold without supervision.

As with all virtues, the teaching towards helpfulness will be greatly enhanced by the parental model.

Explain to your toddler that you are making an extra meal to be helpful to a friend who has just had a baby. Or explain that we are looking after Thomas today to be helpful to his mum. Or that daddy is at a friend's house today to help them with moving to a new house.

Name the virtue, and your child will use that term too. Praise her for being helpful as she finishes a task, and thank her specifically for showing helpfulness. Emphasise how choosing to be helpful, or choosing not to be helpful, will make others feel.

Wisely use these toddler years to introduce your child to the virtue of helpfulness and reap the rewards of this for many years to come.

School Years

There are many ways to organise your children to complete household chores. Chatting to other parents about this will provide various systems. Having a set chore time each day seems to work for many families. During the school years, straight after baths in the early evening seemed to work best. Everyone had their set tasks to do, the cleaning music was playing and it was just part of the daily pattern so the fussing was minimal. You may need to try a few different times of the day and different chore systems that work for you. My children had the same jobs for a term, other parents prefer to change that up weekly or even daily. There is no one right way to approach this. The key is that you are teaching skills and laying the pattern of helpfulness.

Teen Years

I was in a meeting with 200 parents and the speaker asked if we would like to have obedient teens. As parents of young children at the time, many of us thought, 'Yes, of course'. Then this father of 11 (yes, 11) went on to share that we should be aiming for a responsible teen, not an obedient teen. Do you really want to be asking each teen to make their bed each morning for the rest of their life? Or would you like a teen who makes his bed, and completes all his chores independently? That made sense to me. So, I ensured that my teens had more and more responsibility each year. They were encouraged to show initiative and they lost freedoms when they chose not to complete their responsibilities to an acceptable standard and in a timely manner. At age sixteen, they were totally responsible for their own room. Yes, a messy period characterised those first few months of freedom, but so far two out of the three have returned to valuing tidiness. I'm still holding on to hope for the (unnamed) third.

Hebrews 13:16 'Do not neglect to do good and to share what you have, for such is pleasing to God.'

24

Cheerfulness

Cheerfulness – contented, in good spirits, hopeful; bright, pleasant; willing, not reluctant.

Do you think cheerfulness is a virtue that can be taught or is it simply a matter of personality? Do some of your friends have personality types that are more prone to look on the bright side of things, while others tend to focus on the gloomy side?

Each personality type has strengths and weaknesses which can be enhanced by all character training, including training in cheerfulness. You may have a toddler who is full of energy and just really loves to meet people and eagerly anticipates new experiences. Or your toddler may prefer to play alone, is reluctant to mix in large groups and enjoys quiet play. Or maybe somewhere in between.

It is possible to train your child to be cheerful, pleasant and content, regardless of their natural personality type. Personality differences are very real, yes, but they don't excuse extended moods, contrariness, over-reacting and whining. Parental modelling of cheerfulness is a key part of this process. Sound familiar?

I need to be modelling an attitude of contentment toward my role in the home, my household tasks, and my daily plan. I also need to manage my interactions with my child in a pleasant manner. If I don't, then I can't expect this of my child.

Of course, I had my bad days (and my very bad days) from time to time, as did my child. I am not overly cheerful from morning to night, day after day, and I do not expect this of my child either. However, I can make the choice to cheerfully go about my daily tasks and attempt to see the positive side of each situation that comes my way. Likewise, we can gently start to help our toddler to cheerfully go about his daily tasks and begin to help him see the positive side of each situation that comes his way.

Talk about cheerfulness and about having a happy face. Praise your child when you see her playing happily with her toys. Praise her when she packs up with a happy face. Praise her for accepting your choice of morning tea rather than whining for an alternative. Praise her for sitting still while you bathe her rather than squirming and complaining. Whenever you can, praise her for her cheerful and pleasant countenance.

Please note that we are not stifling or denying emotions. Rather, as parents, we can help our children express them in an appropriate manner. A scraped knee, a fall or a bump will be met compassionately with a cuddle and kiss. A sadness or disappointment will be met with concern and sympathy. Tiredness and fatigue will be met with flexibility and understanding.

However, prolonged crying, extended moodiness and constant whining in response to any of the above, does not need to be tolerated. Little by little, you can kindly instruct your child in how to respond in a way that shows self-control and consideration of others. Do not underestimate how much your toddler can understand. You can gently encourage your child to cheerfulness with patience and diligence.

Even an eighteen-month-old is capable of sitting on their bed and coming out when they have replaced their grumpy face with a happy face. Grumpy feelings are not being denied, their expression is simply limited to the bedroom – not out in the family affecting the mood of the whole house.

The proactive and positive teaching of cheerfulness may include the teaching of verses, stories, songs and rhymes that promote a cheerful heart. You could buy some good virtue books or videos, browse the web for helpful sites, borrow ideas from your friends or simply make up your own songs and rhymes.

Some colouring books provide pictures of virtue training, and as you colour a picture together of a happy child, you can be talking about cheerfulness to your child. Or draw your own pictures that depict your child being cheerful in different situations. A scrapbook full of such pictures will delight your child.

Simple games such as charades and musical statues can focus on feelings by making a happy, sad, angry, or surprised face for a turn of charades or when the music stops for musical statues.

Role-plays of various scenarios can also promote cheerfulness and emphasize how the expression of our feelings affects others. Use toys, or puppets, or a cardboard box television, to act out little plays that show fun and a happy face. Keep it very short, maybe limited to just two or three minutes. At first your toddler may not appear to be seeing the reason behind these games, but over time the awareness will grow and this will eventually spill over into everyday situations. Yes, it takes a bit of effort, but it is positive interaction that is lots of fun too. Seeing the changes in your toddler's heart is a beautiful reward for the labour.

As your toddler begins to speak you can have the pleasure of guiding their speech towards pleasant conversation. At meal times, I would ask our little ones about their day and have them share one happy part of the day. As they got older I asked them to share three good things that happened in their day. Then they were to ask another family member about three good things they did in their day, and so on, around the family. This of course can be extended to include the other virtues, e.g. 'Can you name one time today when you were kind?'

Cheerfulness is often the result of contentment. Teaching your child the skill of playing independently will greatly enhance their contentment. A child who is always demanding to be entertained, or spoken to, or who needs a companion for toy play, will not be very cheerful.

I adored playing with my children when they were toddlers (and later too) and we spent plenty of fun times together. However, I also planned small spots in the day for independent play. The purpose of this was for my child to learn to manage playing alone, to be able to enjoy a task without a constant stream of words, and to slowly begin to understand how to be part of a family and not the focus of it. If I did give every single minute of my day to my toddler, then he would rightly perceive himself as more important than anything else in my life. Through a balance of playtime with mum and playtime alone, I was gently communicating to my child that he was an important member of a team, i.e. our family.

Examples of independent play include playpen time or room play, outside play (if your yard is safe), video watching, book reading, activity play at their small table (puzzles, pegs or whatever) or simply playing with toys in a separate room from mum. At first, I planned just a few ten to twenty-minute time slots each day. I would gradually increase this time, little by little, every few weeks or so. By about three years of age they could manage forty to sixty-minute time slots.

These times enable mum to pursue a hobby or interest, spend focus time with another child, and have the household tasks completed without interruption. It also enables mum's friends to interact with her without verbal competition from the toddler.

However, the main benefits are for the child. Providing independent play opportunities every day enables your child to learn to be part of a team, to creatively enjoy themselves and to think of others.

Your toddler will be gaining a great foundation for being part of a group at Pre-School, a Sunday School class, a sporting team, in social situations or for education. He will not be expecting to have the entire focus of the teacher, visitors, or sports coach, either through physical presence or verbal comments.

He will be cheerful, pleasant and content – a pleasure!

School Years

At dinner one night, my five-year-old was deep in thought. I had asked him to share one good thing about his day at school and he was struggling to find that one thing. Finally, his face brightened and he said, 'I wasn't last in line when we walked to the library!' This child naturally struggled to see the good in a day. Yet over the years, as he was consistently asked to share one, then two, and then three good things in each day, he was more readily able to answer this question.

As parents, you can influence your child and it is your calm consistency and personal modelling that are powerful tools in this process.

Teen Years

The teen years provide a myriad of opportunities to practice cheerfulness. Will you guide your child to first be resilient, and then cheerful, when they are not invited to a party, when friendship groups change, when a teacher makes an unfair decision, and when they don't do as well as they expected in that exam, assessment or race?

Later, the bigger issues of romantic relationships, career options denied, unfair treatment in their workplace, dreams of sporting success ended due to injury or illness and the closing of preferred further study options need to be dealt with. Will your teen be able to be realistic and cheerful in the face of disappointment and setbacks, or will they fall into self-pity, anger and depression and engage in selfish, acting-out or withdrawal behaviours? It is the early foundation of training, your calm consistency and your own modelling, that will greatly aid your teen in this area.

Proverbs 17:22 'A cheerful heart is good medicine, but a downcast spirit dries up the bones.'

> *As a child, and even as a teenager, I struggled with self-control. I have always been impulsive (act now and think later) wanting my own way, you know - pretty much your average strong-willed child. My story is different, because I have something that a lot of other kids don't have the privilege of having - My Parents. A woman who loved me enough to set the right kind boundaries for me as a child, and a man who wholeheartedly backed her up and led our family by example.*
>
> *As an adult, I'm now thankful that I was expected to respect authority, to look people in the eye when I speak to them, was taught how to follow instructions with a happy heart (this was a*

rough road for both my mother and myself), to think of others before myself and that being the odd one out isn't a sad thing. I see now that the countless hours mum spent teaching me how to interrupt politely, how to talk to and listen to people of all ages, how to be patient and wait my turn... basically teaching me self-control - was worth every painstaking second.

I've been working in a Hospital since I was 16, showering and toileting patients who can't care for themselves, and there is no way I could have done this if I hadn't had the upbringing that I did. I have had countless comments from co-workers, complimenting me on my maturity, people skills and respect for those around me. They find it hard to believe that I am still a teenager. Even though at 19 I'm considered an adult, I'm still strengthening the self-control my parents taught me as a child, something that I'm sure will be a life-long project. I am, however, extremely thankful for the strong foundation that they have laid in me.

Sam C, age 19

25

Fun

Fun – amusing; entertaining; exciting and enjoyable.

Toddler Years

The toddler years can be some of the most enjoyable of the whole parenting experience. Watching your child grow so rapidly in their verbal and physical development during these years is fascinating. I loved the little phrases that were not quite right, the wonder in the seemingly mundane aspects of life, their pleasure in their own little achievements, the fruit of growing independence and the uniqueness of their emerging personality.

Enjoy this season of your life. Have fun teaching your child to have a happy, healthy heart.

Laugh lots.

Take time for picnics, leisurely walks, mysterious tours, 'midnight' snacks (at 8:00 pm), imaginary play, tea parties and sleep outs in the lounge room. Enjoy ice cream treats, family fun nights, dress ups, pretend photo shoots, charades, movies, bus and train rides and café visits. Enjoy parties, baking, exploring new playgrounds, and eating fish-n-chips on the beach and treasure hunts.

Read the books you yourself enjoyed as a child, tell stories of your own childhood, and creatively establish traditions and fun memories for your child.

School Years

The school years are full of new experiences.

Starting 'big' school, learning to read, writing stories, learning to add and subtract, enjoying art and crafts, learning to hop and skip and play ball games, enjoying birthday parties and family outings, having new experiences on excursions and sports carnival days at school, finding their hobby or sport, developing their sense of fashion, learning more about the world around them, taking an interest in current affairs and developing deeper friendships.

Laugh lots.

Try new things together and make time each day just to chat (not to lecture or instruct) just to share together. Be the parent, not their friend, and let them know how much you value them and how glad you are that they are in your family. Listen well as they share the issues of the day and about the little dramas in their friendships and groups. Encourage their creativity and individuality and be present with them. Enjoy this season.

Teen Years

The teen years are a time of change. They change from boys and girls to young men and women. You slowly transition from being the parent, to being alongside them and encouraging them on the way, and then to friendship.

I love catching up with my adult children for lunch, a game of tennis, a sporting event or a musical. I love chatting to them on the phone and enjoying adventure holidays with them. They are a great delight to my heart and I so enjoy being with them.

The parenting years of Caleb, Emily and Samuel were busy, and of course we had our challenging seasons too. Overall, however, these years were incredibly rewarding and fun.

May you also, greatly enjoy these precious parenting years.

26

Bumps Along the Way

Life is messy.

There will be changes, hardship, challenges and heartbreak along the way.

Bumps along the way may be caused by:

- Changes in work conditions or unemployment
- Proximity and availability of extended family
- Home or Public or Private schooling options
- Church community commitments
- Illness and mental health issues
- Accident or disability
- Renovations and house moves
- The number, ages and spacing of children in the family
- Financial decisions and pressures
- Natural disasters such as flood, fire and storms
- School activities and related issues
- Addictions
- Extra-curricular activities
- Personal hobbies and interests
- Disappointments, failures and expectations
- Family breakdowns
- Friendship changes
- Poor lifestyle choices

Many of these things are out of your control and some will affect your whole family, others will affect just an individual in your family. Some issues are random and unexpected. Preparing your child for the bumps along the way will greatly help them navigate these bumpy seasons. A firm foundation of heart training will give them the best basis from which to face these trials.

I have spoken to hundreds of families over the last twenty years and every single one of them has had a season of challenge. There are bumps on the road of every life journey. Almost every teen or young adult has had a time of choosing their own way, challenging the values they grew up with and testing the freedoms of adulthood. Some of these times have been brief, like a small ripple, others have lasted months and been quite intense, like a stormy sea, and others have lasted years, like a constant angry ocean. It can be heartbreaking, challenging and difficult for the parents.

We are not responsible for the choices of our adult children. We are responsible for teaching them in their childhood years. We do our imperfect best to train them in the right way. Then our active parenting role is done. Our task then is to love them and maintain our relationship with them through the adult years, and then, hopefully, enjoy the privilege of the grandparent stage.

Isaiah 54:10 'Though the mountains be shaken and the hills be removed, yet my unfailing love for you will not be shaken nor my covenant of peace be removed,' says the Lord, who has compassion on you.

27

Cyber-Parenting

James and Simone Boswell – Parents to 6 children, Grandparents to one

Toddlers and Tablets

Technology has come a long way in the last few years!

Once, we could slot 'technology time' into the short television moments of the day. Playschool in the morning, another favourite show in the afternoon and the occasional family movie. But things have changed. Where does technology fit into your home?

Are you spending time on your phone before you get out of bed? Is your laptop on the kitchen table throughout the day for easy access? Is your phone always within reach?

It is definitely a different world now that our technology surrounds us. We make choices all through the day to depend on our own technology to sound alarms, provide weather information and to communicate with our spouse, friends, older children or extended family whenever we need to. We choose music, we play games, we even work from home and answer emails or correspond with colleagues and bosses.

How about our toddlers and young children at home with us? How does technology fit into their world? From tablets which are just the right size for chubby toddler fingers, to easy-access phones in handbags, to gaming consoles -

our children understand that our technology is their technology. Why should we consider how to manage their technology use?

Unregulated technology use can lead to slow language development, delayed fine and gross motor skills, sensory overload, poor eyesight, back and neck pain, and delays in problem solving skills because toddlers may not have the large chunks of creative play they need to stimulate their creative play brains.

How do we make decisions about managing technology around our toddlers?

Here are some suggestions:

Shared play: Play with your child so you can verbally communicate while you play, and they can experience your physical presence and touch.

Age-appropriate play: Carefully review ratings of games and apps so they are age appropriate. Monitor your toddlers and preschoolers around older children's screen time.

Free play: Never allow your preschooler to freely explore the internet. It takes just one click for them to be confronted by an inappropriate image or concept that they will never forget.

Balanced play: Balance screen time with outside time, physical activity, book reading, toys, imaginative play and mummy (daddy, sibling, grandparent) time.

Supervised play: Avoid using screens as babysitters and never allow TVs, computers or mobile devices in bedrooms unsupervised. Always be close to your young child while they are playing on a device.

Safe play: Password lock all screens on mobile devices. Consider locking down internet exploring access on child devices, along with apps such as Youtube, app store etc., so that you remain in control of what your child can access.

It is never too early to think about the impact of technology use on your children. While the temptation is to do what everyone else is doing, your child will benefit from a parent who considers both the benefit and cost of technology use from birth through the teen years.

Be encouraged to make decisions that consider self-control, balance and maturity when it comes to screen time.

School Kids and Devices

Beginning school may add another element of complexity in managing screen time with the introduction of the school iPad.

When it comes to making decisions about how to manage kids and their devices, it's helpful to look at 3 areas: Content, Relationship and Time.

Content

What content is your child consuming when they use their device? Content includes games (like Minecraft), videos (Youtube), movies and TV shows, apps and social media sites.

Does the content they consume on their device reflect your family values? Is it age appropriate? Do you check ratings on games and movies to check that the content is suitable for your child? Is your child using an app which has an age limit? Many primary kids are using popular social media apps (Facebook, Instagram, Snapchat, YouTube, musical.ly etc.) which are designed for teens and adults.

There are definite dangers for children being exposed to the content on these apps - in subject content, images and conversation. Kids are not just consuming content, they are creating content. Status updates, photos, videos and comments - this is all created content. Have you chatted with your kids about taking and uploading appropriate photos and videos? Are you regularly talking about appropriate online conversation?

Relationship

Another area to consider is the area of relationship. How is the screen time use in your house affecting family relationships? Family relationships can be strengthened when families use devices wisely. We can play games with our kids, we can communicate with each other and distant family and we can watch videos and movies together.

Screen time use can also adversely affect family relationships, and the relationships between our kids and the people they are communicating with online. If you have decided that your child is ready to interact with other people online, then you would be wise to have regular conversations with them about how they interact, and how they can avoid contact with strangers.

Time

The third area to consider with children of this age is the time aspect of screen time use. Most kids - and adults - find that time spent on screens can be overwhelming. As a parent, have some boundaries about how much time your child spends online. Even when their device comes home from school for homework, you can monitor how much of their time at home is devoted to screen time, and how much is spent on other activities.

Remember to keep all devices for children in public areas of the house, avoiding the temptation for them to use devices in secret. This allows an element of supervision and an opportunity to engage with your child during their screen time.

Our school aged kids are learning so fast and they are using their devices in ways we haven't imagined. We can marvel at their curiosity and discovery, but also remain firm in keeping clear boundaries to keep them safe while they explore the world online.

Teens and Screens

They were born in the digital age - they are digital natives! They have never known a moment without a screen in sight. Our teens are living a rather different life to us. Is it possible to have boundaries in our homes for our teens and their screens?

Not only is it possible to have boundaries, it is our responsibility to ensure that it happens. Our kids are not going to set their own wise boundaries. While those boundaries change as they get older, and increase to reflect their growing maturity, teens without boundaries quickly find themselves caught up in situations way out of their control.

For many teens, the big issues related to cyberbullying, gaming addiction, social media and pornography become all consuming. While parents can't control every aspect of their online lives, our approach to setting boundaries, supervising and being a part of their world will set the course for these teen years.

Our plan for managing these years involves being informed about what our teens are doing online, teaching them to be wise users of technology, modelling good behaviour, protecting them from harm, supervising their tech use and trusting them to make wise decisions as they mature.

What devices is our teen using? How is he spending his time? Is he on social media? Which social media apps does he use? What games is he playing? What videos does he watch? These are the questions we ask ourselves and our teens as part of being an *informed parent*. Some parents are unwilling to be a part of their teen's online world. Some parents have handed over all manner of connectivity to their child and feel they have no business knowing what they are doing. But parenting continues through the teens years, and hopefully good communication through the toddler and early school years will continue into the teen years, so that parents can have conversations with their teens to help understand their tech world.

Do we have anything to teach our teens about technology? Of course! Not in terms of using technology - they know way more about navigating online spaces than we do - but in terms of teaching them how to make wise decisions. Wise use of time, wise consumption of content and wise words in online conversation. Little by little, over many conversations - both light hearted and deep - using encouragement and occasionally consequences, we *teach* our teens to be positive participators in the online world.

Modelling good habits is always the hardest part of parenting. Are we on our phones too much? Do we watch too much Netflix? Are we as attached to our devices as our teens? Modelling good behaviour is an essential part of parenting, and even more important now they are teens - they are watching everything we do and weighing us up in light of what we require of them. They are now old enough to see how we behave in the online world, so it's a good time to re-evaluate our own choices and make sure that our model is a good model.

A parent's strongest instinct through the early years is to protect our children from harm. We don't let our toddlers play on the freeway, but now they are teens that freeway has become an endless online world. How can we possibly *protect* them from all harm? We can't protect them from all harm, but we can establish boundaries that will help to protect them until they are mature enough to make wise decisions. Password locking devices, age restrictions on social media sites, installing filters on home Wi-Fi and devices are all ways to protect our kids, whether they are young children or teens. Wise parents will use these strategies to protect their children.

When our children are toddlers, we *supervise* their every moment using technology. We can't supervise every moment of our teen's world, however, we can keep a general eye on how they use their time by establishing some boundaries. Encourage your teens to be a part of the family by being in family areas of the house to play games or do homework, rather than always being locked away in their room. Sign up to Facebook, Instagram or another social media site where your child has a presence. Accountability software is very helpful for older teens, who may be tempted to explore dark places online.

Our toddlers become school kids. Our school kids become teenagers. Our teenagers become young adults. We don't want to be still closely monitoring their every move by the time they are ready to leave home! Our boundaries and freedoms must be released as they grow older, so they can make small mistakes early on and learn from them, and avoid hard-to-live-with mistakes when they are young adults. We need to *trust* them that they will mature and will learn to make wise decisions without our constant direction.

The teen years can be challenging but they can also be terrific. Our children grow in maturity before our eyes and turn into adults. At every stage of the parenting journey through the world of technology, we can adapt and change as they grow into kind and wise people who shine into the online world in which they live.

28

Dad to Dad

Geoff Bongers – Dad to 4 teens

Understanding

One thing you learn early on as a Dad is that all your kids are different, from how athletic they are, whether they are ticklish or not, how introverted or not they are, through to how they respond to encouragement, correction, disappointment and challenges. What's important about that is the need to understand your own personality and character, and how that impacts your interactions with your kids. In this teenage stage, knowing who likes to sit and talk, have a playmate in the back yard or that extra hug or encouraging word when doing that tough school assignment or task is very important to ensure you speak love in a way that's understood.

Talking

I have found, however, that most teens like to talk. Some of the discussions around the dinner table, on the way home from some activity or other, or just before I'm ready to go to bed have been great. Importantly these are often grown up versions of the 'windows of the heart' opportunities I had with them when they were younger. The trust built up when they were younger by not 'just fixing it' and listening, has allowed these deeper conversations now.

Transitions

Another thing you learn as a Dad, is that nothing stays the same for long. The cute bundle of hugs who loved sitting on your lap 'not that long ago' is now that 'teen' learning how to drive. This means transitions happen all the time and they need to be managed and worked through. There are many times my wife and I had to work through what these new freedoms meant and the new boundaries – this was not always easy and we did not always agree or see it exactly the same way. This sometimes meant a set of 'trial conditions' for a new freedom.

Freedoms

Granting new freedoms doesn't seem to get much easier – as the failure options and resulting consequences get bigger too . . . crashing the car, failing a university or TAFE subject, being a poor example as a junior helper or youth leader, losing a job because they are late etc. However, helping the kids learn from near misses or failures is a key opportunity to do some high value parenting. Coming alongside after failure, to see what can be learnt from it all and what could be done differently next time, is a source of valuable life lessons and character refinement. All of this has been possible and effective because it has been built upon years of being trusted with granting freedoms and working through transitions from a young age.

Too Busy

Finally, a word about being busy . . . It is extremely easy for dads to miss so much because of work, church, sport and other 'important things'. Your kids will grow up fast – believe it or not, it's a short season we have them in our direct care. Don't miss being a significant influence by being too busy. Take time to interact one-on-one and as a family.

Andy Hamdorf – Dad to 3 adult children

Loving Leadership

The phrase that sums it all up; 'Man up and take point!' What I want to say with that is that we simply need to take the responsibility we have as dads squarely on our shoulders. There are so many temptations and reasons to let things slip but I want to encourage you to persevere because the rewards are so worth the effort, and besides, what would the alternative be? Ultimately our desire is to have a positive influence on the lives of our kids. Influence is based on the power of the relationship we have, relationship is built on trust, trust is established from respect, and respect is earned when we live as men of character - Godly character. Dads are called to lead their families as men of Godly character, that's the starting point, and in the words of Arnie. . . 'Just do it. . .do it now'.

Everything we do as dads has a benefit and a cost. We can't have all the benefits without paying any of the costs, everything has a price. The question we need to ask ourselves is, 'What price are we willing to pay for the benefits we want to achieve?' What price are you paying right now, and what are you getting for that price?

A Great Husband First

It goes without saying that the initial point I would like to emphasize is that dads need to first be great husbands. Since healthy marriage is a topic that has been the subject of many, many books I can't say too much except that if you are experiencing difficulties in your marriage then I urge you to seek help. This doesn't have to wait until there are serious problems. In fact, I suggest that even healthy married couples should regularly involve themselves in some sort of marriage enrichment program or study. We just need the encouragement and the timely reminders to stay on track and do well.

Consistency

One of the hardest things to do is to be consistent in our parenting. To speak words of life all the time, to hold the kids to the same standard and to hold ourselves to the same standard. Even after a bad day at work or when disappointment strikes. There is no simple answer to doing it. It takes practice and time and you have to be intentional but you can do it.

Making Decisions for the Family before Career

To do all of this you can't do it well if you are an absent husband and dad. Yes, some of us have jobs where we have to travel. I have several friends who do, and they do a good job of balancing the travel and their family life, but there is no substitute for being there all the time. I had a time in my career where I would work away for 3 months at a time, coming home 1 weekend in 4. I loved the money and the accolade I had for the work I was doing BUT it was affecting the security of my kids. For this reason, I chose family over big dollars. Yes, it was harder financially but my family needed me. Even today the kids still talk of how I sacrificed that work for them.

Peter Foote – Dad to 4, ages 10 – 19

When 'Yes, Dad' Can Sometimes Be Bad

With three of our children in the teen years (13, 16 and 19) I've been doing a lot of reflecting lately on which aspects of our parenting have borne fruit and which have not. As a dad who tends towards routine and order, I've been realising lately that some aspects of my parenting style were not good.

The most painful example for me is not relying enough on the Holy Spirit before giving instructions. There were many times, especially in the teen years, when something was going on in the heart of my child, but I was busy, or focused on other things or simply just not paying attention. So, when I gave my instruction, it ignored the issue they were wrestling with and turned them into a robot i.e. 'Yes, Dad', even though it wasn't from the heart.

This is not an issue with obedience, as the Bible talks about children obeying their parents. It is about me thinking that I can simply apply a formula to my child, regardless of the context, and all will be well. The human heart is a mystery and requires spiritual insight to nurture it properly.

It reminds me of John 3:8, 'The wind blows wherever it pleases. You hear its sound, but you cannot tell where it comes from or where it is going. So, it is with everyone born of the Spirit'. I needed to be listening to the Holy Spirit more, who knew exactly what was going on in the heart of my child.

I also needed to have the attitude of Jesus, who was totally dependent on His Father for everything He did. One of my favourite verses on this is John 15:5, 'I am the vine; you are the branches. If a man remains in me and I in him, he will bear much fruit; apart from me you can do nothing'. No matter how well I apply the teachings of Growing Families, if I am not relying on Jesus, I will bear little fruit that lasts into eternity.

The good news is that God is a way better Father than I am, and in His grace and by His Spirit, He is working in the hearts of my children to heal the wounds I have caused and to draw them to Himself as their TRUE Father (I am just a shadow of

His AMAZING reality). Both my children and I are learning to bring our brokenness to God and allow Him to heal it.

As we seek to love Him and each other, He lays a foundation in our lives that lets us weather our brokenness and the storms that life brings. And that foundation, the ONLY true foundation, is the love of God expressed through Jesus.

From a broken and healing dad, Peter

29

How the Story Ends

I am so thankful to have known Jesus for almost all my life. He is my Rock, my strength, my source of wisdom, my joy, my hope and my peace. I long to know, love and serve Him with all that I do every day. He has been with me in the dry, hard seasons, the normal, mundane seasons, and in the fruitful, good seasons.

My Bible is rich food for thought and my guidebook for living. I believe what the Bible says when it describes this life as temporary. We live for maybe 70 or 80 years or so on this earth, then we will live forever in eternity. As a parent, I prepare my children to be wise, content, productive and respectful adults.

My biggest task, however, is to prepare my children for eternity. I do not make that decision for them, but I can diligently fill their hearts with virtues that reflect God's character and gently point them to Him. I can teach them the right way and the right reasons, and equip them with the self-control to choose to do right along the way.

My greatest anticipation is at the thought of that momentous moment when I will actually see my Jesus face-to-face for the first time. I think often, almost daily, of that magnificent day, and I eagerly long for that day to come.

The only thing greater than that moment, will be standing there with my precious three children, and their wonderful spouses and their treasured children, by my side.

Knowing how the story ends, living forever in eternity with Him, makes all the difference to my parenting journey. It is worthy of much energy, time, sacrifices, prayers and love.

> Upon reflection on how my childhood has impacted me later in life, three points immediately come to mind.
>
> Firstly, I now realise how much of an impact having a consistent routine has had on my life. I've found it helpful to have a tendency for structure and planning in my days, whether it be studying, working or resting. Yes, even on holidays and weekends, I find myself at least subconsciously making a plan for the day to ensure that the things I need, or want, to get done actually get done. Routine has taught me discipline, and it has been helpful to have that platform established early on in life to make sure I can set aside time to read my Bible and pray, exercise, and do household chores, even on work days.
>
> Secondly, I don't know how this happened, but I still remember, very clearly, being taught the Bible at a very young age. Some verses (and songs) are just so ingrained in my head I don't think I will ever forget them. I have found this useful in times when I don't know what to pray, read or even think. Sometimes a verse or a song from my childhood will just pop to the front of my mind and it will refresh me!
>
> Lastly, sleep. I've been pretty good at sleeping for as long as I can remember. Several friends, teachers and work colleagues have commented on how I am always refreshed and energetic throughout the whole day. It's because I sleep! Definitely a flow-on from routine; planning to have an adequate amount of sleep has been incredibly helpful. I definitely take it for granted sometimes, but I appreciate having loads of energy to get through the day.
>
> Mum, I greatly admire how much you strive to keep learning spiritually and academically and how selfless your pursuits in life are.

You live out John 15:12 so well. Thank you for always being supportive and super helpful. I hope we continue to be close for the rest of our years through all of the trials, tests and happy moments. You also seem to be doing less embarrassing things which is good to see. Love you heaps.

Caleb Hayde, age 23

'Point your kids in the right direction. When they're old they won't be lost.' Proverbs 22:6

The virtues of self-control, patience and respect which have been instilled in me through my childhood, have helped me flourish in my jobs as an adult, my relationships with my friends and my relationship with Jesus.

'For it is pleasing when you keep them in your heart and have all them ready on your lips.' Proverbs 22:18

My mum's Christ-focused parenting allowed me to grow up always knowing Jesus and His love. It wasn't forced which then allowed me to come to a relationship with Jesus on my own.

Some kids are given everything. If they are told 'No', they throw a tantrum and it's like it is the end of the world. Growing up I was given a healthy balance, which has allowed me to be resilient and deal with having to work my way around situations.

Thank you SO much, Mum, for your incredible sacrifices and for demonstrating God's love. I love you so much.

Sam Hayde, age 19

The Hands that Held
by Emily Hayde, age 22

The hands that held me,
those that led,
Gently, tightly and so secure.
Keeping me safe,
Then guiding me on,
Then letting go.

Your hands that held me,
those that led,
now they let me go,
gently, softly and feeling secure.

The words that taught me,
those that showed,
Comforting, wise and trustworthy.
Keeping me loved,
Then showing me on,
Then keeping quiet.

Your words that taught me,
those that showed,
Now are in my heart,
Comforting, wise and still trustworthy.

The path that led me,
that which lit,
Brightly, rightly and so of God.
Keeping me on the way,
Then holding me there,
Then stepping back.

The path that led me,
that which lit,
Now is my chosen path,
Brightly, rightly and so of God.

Your hands held me,
your words taught me,
Your path led me,
To God.

Now His hands, they hold me,
His words, they teach me,
His path, His alone, leads me.

And as I live in and with Him,
I am reminded of His love
And of you.
For His hands, words and path,
Remind me of yours.

30 Questions

Activities

1. There are so many activities available for our children. How do I choose what to do?

This is purely a matter of personal preference. When they were quite young they had one activity in the week (playgroup, kindy gym or music playtime) and church on Sunday.

During the school years, I aimed to have one sport activity for each child and they each had a season of learning a musical instrument. In early high school, they added Youth Group at church each Friday night and then later they added a part-time job. Some families manage more, others less. It's your choice.

Anger

2. I think it is appropriate to show my children when I am angry with them. When I yell and scream they certainly know that I am cross. Is this okay?

Two things to think about.

Firstly, do the actual words you use during your outburst ridicule or esteem your child? It is very important to express our displeasure at our child's actions, and not them as a person. We love who they are, but we don't always love what they do.

Secondly, it is important to realise that our children listen far more to our actions than our words. We model to them how to cope with anger. They are watching and learning how we relate to our spouse, peers, and to them, especially in conflict situations.

Do we yell, scream and shout or do we calmly and rationally present our honest view? They will model our behaviour back to us. Think ahead, do you want a teenager who yells when angry or one who can calmly talk an issue through?

By the time Caleb was twelve years old, he, at times, strongly disagreed with a decision we had made for him. He had enough self-control to sit and discuss an issue with me. If things got a little tense, then he, or I, would suggest a little break for a few minutes until we were able to discuss it calmly again. My heart was deeply touched by this and it gave me great hope for the years ahead. I wish I had been able to deal with conflict in this way during my younger years.

Boy Behaviours

3. I want my little boy to be a boy and do boy things – not to be sitting and concentrating all day.

Digging in the garden, hammering with wood and nails, making mud pies, playing and splashing with water, chasing the dog, climbing trees, building cubby houses and rockets out of boxes, playing rough-n-tumble with dad, zooming around on bikes and playing with bats and balls are all fun activities for little boys. Do include lots of these in your outside play and family fun times (supervised of course!). Balancing these types of activities with small times of focusing skills provides variety to his day and will greatly enhance your son's overall development.

Character Issues

4. I'm feeling a little overwhelmed as I see so many character issues I want to work on with my toddler. Where should I start?

Remember that you have eighteen years to parent and you do not have to work on everything today. Maybe focus on self-control and obedience first, as all the other virtues will benefit from having these in place.

Choose only one or two issues to work on at a time. Maybe write them out and place the note where you can refer to it regularly to keep you focused. The purpose of this book is to present a few practical ways you can train character virtues into the heart of your toddler.

The ideas are suggestions only, and hopefully they will stimulate your own ideas that are more appropriate for your individual family. Then, of course, you can continue to positively guide and train your child at every age!

Choices

5. Thank you, so much, for all your advice on proactively training my toddler. I've now implemented a flexible routine into my day. I was sceptical at first but the changes have been amazing. We still have little battles over what to do during each activity (e.g. I'll choose the crayons and she'll want the pencils for drawing time). Can I minimise these?

I'm so pleased to hear that things have improved for you. Do remember that while a flexible pattern will not prevent all your battles, it will provide an environment to help you proactively teach and train your children.

I suggest that you make all the decisions for your 2-year-old. When she can generally accept your decisions then you can start to give her limited choices, for example the Wiggles or Hooley Dooley's video for TV time.

As the mum, you probably don't mind which video of the two she may choose, and feel quite ambivalent about the issue. However, it is the decision-making process and not the object of the choice that is crucial to your child. If she makes lots of decisions, she will feel that she is in charge and will therefore constantly question your authority all day.

Chores

6. Isn't it expecting too much to have a two-year-old help around the house? Won't this come naturally later?

Remember that training is happening whether you actively plan for it or not. It is much easier to have your toddler doing one or two little jobs at this stage and then gradually increase his responsibilities. This way he will be learning that he is a productive member of the family right from the start of his memory. To suddenly expect your six or seven-year-old to do some chores is much harder as he has already been indirectly taught that mum and dad do all the work.

Concentration

7. My two-year-old girl is full of energy and never stops bouncing. How can I ever teach her to sit still and concentrate in time for Pre-School and School?

Firstly, do ensure that you provide lots of positive outlets for this energy in vigorous play and active chores. Alternate your day between quiet activities and active ones. Keep your focusing activities very, very short.

For example, you may start with only three minutes of reading time after lunch and then slowly build that time up. Be patient and consistent and stretch a little each day.

Demand-Attention

8. My almost three-year-old does not let me talk on the phone, converse with visitors or have a few uninterrupted minutes to read a magazine. She is constantly asking me to play with her. What can I do to change this behaviour?

This child is thinking only of herself. You need to gradually teach her that she is part of a family, not the focus. To do this you need to ensure you balance her activities to include times where she plays alone (e.g. outside play, room play, video watching, pre-school activity books and free play) and these times in her day will give her the skills to play happily alone and not to be so demanding and self-focused.

Maybe aim for about a third of her day to be filled with activities she can do independently. Take the time to show her how to play with her toys and give her ideas of how to play alone.

Ensure that you have age appropriate toys for her – a three-year-old is much more advanced than a two-year-old.

Decisions

9. My teen is struggling to make a decision about their future career. What can I do?

This is very common. Looking through a University or TAFE information booklet can help them identify fields they have an interest in. Online tests can suggest areas of aptitude and compatibility with their particular gifts and strengths. Encourage them to talk to friends and family in various careers so they can get a close-up view of the reality of various professions.

Dinner

10. Meal times are horrible with my two boys. They are loud, they fight and they will not sit still for the whole meal. I would like my mealtimes to be pleasant and filled with happy conversation. Should I just give up?

Mealtime behaviour is often a reflection of what is happening during the rest of the day. Tighten up your routine and make sure you are making all the decisions for your boys during the day.

They should only have one or two free play times at this age. As you work on self-control, through play, each day, you will have more pleasant meal times.

Maybe leave your own meal to eat in peace later and be available to train. Work on one thing at a time. For example, you may first work on teaching them to be quiet.

Clearly state your expectation, 'There will be no talking until you have finished your meal'.

Also, clearly state the consequences for compliance or disobedience. Rewards may include a sticker on a chart (5 stickers for a small toy) or dessert (a healthy one of course).

Isolation, no dessert or simply putting them to bed for the night (with a drink first) may motivate your boys to obey. If you are calm and consistent, you will see changes.

Dinner

11. My school aged child is very vocal about their opinion of the food served for dinner. Most of these comments are quite negative. How can I change this pattern?

Simply state that the only comments allowed about the food are ones that thank the chef for their time and effort, and ones that are complimentary about the flavours. Any other comments will result in removal from the table. Also, having your school aged child prepare a meal each week will help them appreciate how much effort dinner takes.

Feelings

12. Some days I am a calm parent, other days I scream all day. Some days I feel quite happy and positive, other days I struggle with the emotions of fear and guilt and doubt and worry. How can I manage this better?

Our feelings scream at us to be obeyed. They are loud, overbearing and persistent. Acknowledge them, be honest about them, but do not be controlled by them. Do the next thing in your day, regardless of how you feel, and base your decisions on lasting facts, not just the intensity of the emotion of the moment.

Issues

13. I have a great pattern for my day, and am really enjoying my week now, yet I am still dealing with two or three issues with my toddler. Is that normal?

Yes! There will always be something to work on for the next eighteen years – this is simply part of parenting! Having a routine will minimise the number of issues you will need to deal with at any one time, but it will not eliminate them. Having only two or three issues to deal with shows that your routine is quite appropriate for your child.

In fact, if you didn't have any training points in your day then you would know your routine is too tight. So, you would increase the time you allow for each activity and also give your toddler more free-time during each day. Keep adjusting until you feel it is working well.

Issues

14. I am really struggling with . . . we have been working on this particular behaviour for months without seeing any improvement. I have been calm and consistent with my praise and consequences. It is driving me crazy. Please help.

If your toddler is going toe-to-toe with you on one issue, then you need to look at the big picture. It is normally an indication that your overall day is too loose for that particular child.

You need to tighten up your routine. If your day has been divided into one-hour time slots, then tighten it up to 30 – 40 minutes per activity. Watch the transition time between activities. Have your child sit and wait until you are both ready to move on; don't allow him 5 –15 minutes of aimless wandering around.

Ensure you are making the hundreds of little decisions each day that relate to your child. Are you expecting self-control in all areas of the day, or only in those areas that maybe embarrass or frustrate you? Are you out more than you are at home?

The best environment for training is in the home. Are you and your husband parenting on the same page? The efforts of the stay-at-home parent can be undermined, or greatly strengthened, by the attitude and support of the spouse.

If you are consistently teaching self-control in all areas of your day within the framework of a routine, if you are home most days and if you are making all the decisions for your toddler, then you have the right environment to work on this issue.

Gradually increase your positive and negative consequences when you deal with this behaviour. Apply them immediately, calmly and consistently. Be patient. You will have good days and bad days, but you should be seeing gradual improvement from week to week. You will reap fruit if you diligently sow.

Late Afternoon

15. I seem to manage okay with most of my day, but I'm finding that from after 5:00 pm each afternoon it's chaos. I yell at the kids and I always feel guilty afterwards, how can I stop this happening?

You firstly need to evaluate your pattern for the entire day. Ensure the morning and early afternoon is filled with a variety of activities that are fun for the child and are also instilling self-control.

Also make sure you get a little rest time early afternoon. If I had just half an hour to myself after lunch, then I was usually refreshed enough to last to the end of the day – when I didn't get that little break I was inclined to get grumpy.

Then just experiment a little with your evening routine. A quiet video just before dinner, reading or a puzzle in separate rooms (particularly if they are prone to fight at this time of the day) or drawing at the kitchen table are all options for when you are cooking dinner.

Try to bath either before dinner prep or after dinner is over to minimise your stress. Have the same ritual for bedtime each night (e.g. teeth, toilet, story, prayers, and lights out). Be encouraged, you can have calm and peaceful evenings.

Motivation

16. My school aged child is simply not motivated to do his homework or study for his exams. How can I help him?

Ensure you have a flexible pattern for your entire week. Having a regular time for school work will help create the habits needed for academic success. Talk to your child about doing what is right even though they might not feel like it. Allow him to experience the logical consequences the school imposes for non-completion of tasks. Do not try to lighten these for him. Experiencing the full weight of the consequences will help him see the link between his choices and the results of those choices.

Choosing to do right, despite strong feelings, is a sign of both maturity and character development and hence is well worth fostering.

Night-Time Sleep

17. My three-year-old will not stay in bed at night. We have a story and a long cuddle before I say goodnight, but she will be up within five minutes. This can go on and on for an hour or two each night. I would like, and really need, my evenings to be uninterrupted for myself.

First, examine if your daughter is going to bed at the right time. Too early and she will not be tired enough to sleep, too late and she will be overtired and will have difficulty putting herself to sleep. All toddlers are different, but somewhere between 6:00 pm and 8:00 pm seems to suit most.

A flexible pattern for your day will provide the framework for you to proactively teach your daughter self-control. It is self-control that enables a toddler to stay in bed all night. As you work on her self-control all day, every day, through the fun play activities, your daughter will learn to stay in bed.

Also think through your response each time your daughter gets out of bed. You need to have a very calm consequence that is meaningful to your child. Reward her first thing in the morning if she has managed to stay in bed. Praise her appropriate choice and be very positive.

Also ensure that your child is seeing mum and dad interacting together as a couple daily. This promotes security and confidence and allows the child to sleep peacefully.

No

18. I have never had a problem with . . . before now, but all of a sudden, we are getting a 'No'. What is happening?

This is not at all surprising. As your child grows he will test boundaries for the first time, or re-test the old boundaries from time to time, sometimes challenging issues you thought you had resolved months ago. If you are calm and firm, with immediate consequences, the battle should be short-lived. He needs to be reassured that mum and dad are in charge, and he will feel secure and happy if the parental expectations are consistent from day to day.

No

19. My 15-month-old is constantly touching the stereo and I feel like I am saying 'No' all day. Please help.

Two things will help here. The first is a flexible pattern for your day. Have a look at the suggestions in this book and adapt it to your needs. A toddler will only have one or two lots of free time each day so they can't even be near the stereo most of the day. Hence you will have a lot less 'No' in your day.

When your child does have free play, ensure you are available to train them. If you immediately isolate them for 5 – 10 minutes you will probably only have 2 or 3 instances of 'No' for that time and then you move on to the next activity in your day.

If you have a pattern for your day, and you have been consistently and calmly applying consequences for a particular behaviour, then you need to look at increasing your consequence. Try 10 – 20 minutes of isolation each time. Give lots of praise for playing with their toys and not touching the stereo.

Nothing to Do

20. My school aged child complains that they have nothing to do if they are not in front of a screen. How can I help them play creatively?

I would give my school aged child 5 minutes to find something productive to do before I would allocate a chore for them to do. Surprisingly, they were always able to think of something!

Do ensure you have art and craft supplies for creative expression, pens and paper for drawing and writing stories, building blocks and groups of toys such as trains, animals, dolls and bears for imaginative play and outside toys for active play.

Also have lots and lots and lots of books available for enjoying and learning.

No

21. When I say 'No' to my 18-month-old girl, she stops what she is doing but then goes straight to another 'No' situation. I will say, 'Stop playing with the phone', and she will, but then go straight to the video player. I will say, 'Stop playing with the video', and she will, but then goes to the drawers. It is a constant cycle until I can distract her or feed her.

Do ensure you have a flexible pattern for your day. You want to minimise the amount of time your little one is able to simply roam around. Redirect her to her own toys by encouraging her towards her dolls or bears. This will be more pleasant for both of you.

Saying 'no' does not motivate your child to change. You need to give her a reason to obey. Toddlers will not respond to the reasoning of words. They will respond to concrete consequences. Lots of cuddles and kisses or small treats when she is not touching these things will be motivating. A quiet but firm no with 5 – 15 minutes of isolation in her cot would also be motivating.

No

22. I am saying 'No' every day to the same issues. For example, I have to remind my three-year-old daughter not to touch the flowers in my garden every time she is outside. It is all rather tedious. What can I do?

A 'No' does not motivate a child to change. Concrete positive and negative consequences motivate behaviour. Add some meaning to your instruction by following it up with a positive reward for compliance or a negative response for disobedience.

If you are calm and consistent with the appropriate reaction, you will see a change.

Also note that your toddler is most capable of remembering from day to day. If you choose every morning to give your child four warnings before following through on a consequence, then you can be sure she will touch the flowers at least four times every day. Respond the first time each morning.

Obedience

23. My daughter has just turned one year of age. Is she too young to learn to obey my instructions?

Not at all! Keep it very simple and fun. Maybe just ask her a few times a day to 'Come to mummy', and reward her with a lovely big tickle and hug. It is much more positive to be proactive in this training, rather than wait until a situation arises in which you need her to obey.

Obedience

24. When I say 'No' to my 14-month-old she just laughs at me and does it anyway. If I smack her hand, she barely cries and still does what she chooses. I'm nervous she will hurt herself if she continues to touch dangerous things. How can I help her obey me?

Read back over the chapter on what motivates a child to obey. A 14-month-old is just starting to test the boundaries and this is very normal. 5 – 15 minutes of isolation can be quite effective for disobedience at this age. For her own safety, she needs to learn that a 'No' from mummy is often protecting her from danger.

Also give lots and lots and lots of praise for compliance. Encouragement is a great motivation for us all.

Outside Play

25. My 10-year-old son never wants to spend any time outside. I lived outside as a child, and want my son to enjoy the benefits of fresh air and an active lifestyle. How can I encourage outside play?

Ensure that he has outside play at the same time every day. This will help minimise the complaining and arguing. Ensure you have age appropriate activities for this time.

Soccer goals, a basketball hoop, bats and balls, bikes and scooters, flower and vegetable patches, woodworking and other outdoor crafts and water play activities may appeal to your son.

Personality

26. Can you allow for unique personality differences in virtue training?

Absolutely! Each child is a unique personality. Each child will respond differently to your instructions. One child may require a firm tone, while another is more responsive to a gentler voice.

One child will battle you in an area that their sibling never did, or the reverse. One child will require three instructions on an issue, while another child will require three hundred instructions on that same issue. One child will really struggle with showing kindness, while another child will struggle with patience. Every child is a one-of-a-kind.

However, each personality type can be enhanced. There will be aspects of each child's personality that you want to minimise, and other parts that you will encourage to develop. The patient teaching of character virtues will greatly improve your child's character and enable his personality to be the best it can be.

Playtime

27. My 15-month-old daughter has recently started to cry during her room playtime. We have been consistent every day and she is not ill or teething. What's happening?

It's probably due to one of two factors. Once children begin to walk they may temporarily not enjoy their room play because they want to be out exploring and practicing their new skill. You may shorten room playtime for a little while but don't disregard it altogether, toddlers still need to focus and concentrate at times, and I'm sure you still need that break for your shower or to do a few chores.

It may also be due to your daughter's growing awareness of self and her expression of that. From this age, you start to get the 'No' for many things and this may be one. Calmly and consistently continue with room playtime and she should settle down in a few weeks. Ensure the toys are age appropriate and that there are only 3 – 4 toys in the room. Playing the same music tape until its end or having a timer for the finish may help.

Positive Consequences

28. I love the idea of using positive consequences rather than nagging or screaming. Are they effective?

Positive consequences are extremely effective within the context of an organised day. For example, if you only have one video time each day, your toddler will quickly learn that it is more fun to sit and watch the video for twenty minutes, rather than to sit in a cot for twenty minutes.

It is also vital to use an even, calm voice (never loud or impatient), as an angry, frustrated tone will incite a similar response in your toddler whereas a gentle, quiet tone will often turn away anger.

Also remember to be consistent every single time, every day.

Praise

29. I am not a naturally positive person. I find it hard to find things to praise my children about. How can I improve in this area?

Thank you for your honest question. You may be surprised just how many mums struggle to be positive amid their busy days.

Plan a short one-to-one time with each child. Regardless of what activity you do together (let the child choose, e.g. books or dolls) you plan on saying three positive things to your child.

For example, 'I love you', 'You are very special to me', or 'I'm so glad God gave you to our family'.

If they do something half right, then praise the good ('You remembered to put your cup on the sink, well done!') and ignore the rest (the plate still on the table!) Use mealtimes to share what each person likes about another family member.

Start by saying one positive comment for every negative or corrective comment. Then build up slowly until you are characterised by being three or four more times as positive. Your child will thrive on your praise.

Routine – Flexible Pattern

30. Do I have to plan a strict pattern for my four and six-year-old? When can they plan their own day?

No! You will be able to gradually loosen your pattern as your child shows more and more self-control. Your six-year-old may even be able to write out his own plan (with a bit of guidance from mum or dad) for getting his tasks done before and after school!

Remember that the pattern is simply a tool that provides a framework within which you can effectively teach and balance your day. I'm sure most successful adults have a personal plan for achieving their goals each day!

Routine – Flexible Pattern

31. I am the mother of a 2-year-old boy and a 4-year-old girl. Every day is chaotic, noisy and messy. I'm exhausted and I am not enjoying them. I feel they have so much that needs working on. Is it too late to start training them? Where do I start?

Firstly, please be assured that it is not too late to start. It will be challenging work, but it will be much easier to start today, than it will be to start in 12 months' time. I often told myself that it must be easier to work with the toys and tantrums of a 2-year-old child, than it is the toys and tantrums of a teen!

Start with establishing a flexible pattern for your day. Write it out and put it up where you can refer to it easily. The first few days will be hard but you should be noticing improvements by the end of the first week.

Once your days are relatively organised, start working on just one behaviour at a time. Don't frustrate your child, or yourself, by trying to change too many things at once. I usually target obedience first because that overlaps to almost every other problem area. If you calmly and consistently work on one frustration at a time, you will see progress, over time.

Don't forget to look after yourself too. Make sure you give yourself breaks each day, and have some fun times planned each week, just for you.

Routine – Flexible Pattern

32. I have spent the last three days trying to organise my day into a pattern. It is not working. My toddler seems more defiant and I'm exhausted. I am ready to give up.

Implementing a flexible pattern into your day will be hard work. Your toddler will seem worse at first. It will take between 3 days and 3 weeks for you to see the fruit of this change. Maybe even a little longer.

Ensure you have a positive tone and over-praise your child for everything during this initial stage. Put all but the essential household chores on hold. Plan to stay home for 3 – 5 days to get your routine established. Have very quick and simple meals planned.

Evaluate your responses – are your rewards and consequences sufficiently motivating your child's behaviour? Re-read all the benefits of a pattern for both yourself and your toddler. Those breaks during the day for yourself are well worth working for. A happy and contented toddler will bring you much joy. Focus on the future. Success is just a few weeks away.

Routine – Flexible Pattern

33. I really struggle with sticking to a routine. I just think I am not a routine person.

The key to sticking to a pattern is to focus on the benefits that result. Can you get all your household chores done, have time for play and fun with your child and have time for yourself each day without a plan?

Also, keep modifying your pattern until it suits your own individual family needs and circumstances. It needs to be your own personal routine for your own family, not a copy of someone else. Do include lots of variety within the day, for you and your toddler, lots of regular social times with other mums and children, and remember spontaneous fun days are essential too!

One family I know simply block out a few hours each week for fun times. They don't decide until that day what to do as mum and dad enjoy the spur of the moment pleasure and freedom of choice amongst the regularity of the weekly chores and responsibilities.

Rudeness

34. My 13-year-old teenage daughter is just rude. She demands that I get this and that for her, never helps out around the house and only thinks of herself. How can I change this pattern?

Ensure that she is doing her own washing and ironing, making her own breakfast, preparing and packing her own lunch for school and making her own snacks. Also give her the responsibility of cleaning her own room, washing and changing her own sheets and keeping her bathroom clean and tidy. Give her one night a week to cook for the family and give her a list of chores to be completed each week.

This will help her contribute to the family rather than just take from it. Failure to comply will result in a loss of freedoms such as outings with friends, weekly allowance and screen time. Your respectful and firm expectations, coupled with the calm and consistent application of consequences, will reap change.

Sharing Toys

35. My day is fairly organised and so my three little ones are mostly happy and content. However, they seem to fight a lot over outside toys. How do I teach them to share?

Do be aware that this is a process that will take some time. Ensure you are free during this activity of the day so you don't feel frustrated by any interruption. When you hear the squeal, intervene straight away. Using a firm, quiet voice, talk them through the situation. I taught my children to say 'No thanks' rather than squeal. If the other child doesn't respond to that polite plea, then the child can come to an adult for assistance.

At first, I aimed for them to simply take short turns with a toy and not to grab from the other. A timer can be very useful here initially. If one child refuses to cooperate, then they simply lose the freedom of playing with their friend, or that toy, or both, for that day.

Shyness

36. My toddler is very shy with strangers and visitors. Should I expect her to say hello?

Have her first practice saying 'Hello' to Daddy, and other people she is very comfortable with, at appropriate times. Praise her for being kind to Daddy and making him feel happy by saying 'Hello'.

Remind her just before you meet someone new that she can say 'Hello' to be kind to that person. Ask her once to say 'Hello' when you are with the visitor, and then just move on with the conversation. Don't ask over and over. By five or six years of age you should expect this basic courtesy, and maybe at this age have a consequence if necessary.

Sibling Friendship

37. My toddler and pre-schooler fight and annoy each other for most of the day. How can I have some peace in my day?

First, organise your day into a flexible pattern. You want to balance out the time your children spend together and apart.

This will help minimise your frustration and you can plan their times together for when you are free from chores and can proactively teach them how to share and how to resolve their little conflicts.

They can be apart during room time (if they share a room for sleeping simply have one of them use your room for this playtime). One child can watch a short video while you have a fun focus time with the other child and then swap them over.

One child can do a quiet activity up at the table while one child has outside play. If they do have times apart each day then they are more likely to appreciate and enjoy the times they are together.

Sibling Friendship

38. I have always wanted my children to be best friends throughout their childhood and into adulthood. Is this just wishful thinking?

Definitely not! This is one of my most cherished parenting desires. Tell your children right from the beginning that they are best friends. Encourage them to love each other through kind words, short notes, little gifts, hugs and kisses, little acts of service and interest in each other's activities. You can foster these precious relationships.

Social Skills

39. My child is over-bearing in social situations. How can I teach her to be a little less dominant?

Social skills are not natural, they will need to be taught to your child. Gently explain to her what you expect before visitors arrive. Keep it short – maybe only two or three expectations at first. Then do ensure you are close by to demonstrate what to do when, and to closely supervise.

It will take practice before she can independently handle these situations. Don't expect too much too soon and keep your guidance as positive as you can.

Stealing

40. My eight-year-old has starting stealing things from school and from her friends. What can I do?

Have a chat to your daughter over an ice-cream or milkshake one afternoon and see if she can tell you why this is happening. Each time it does happen, take the object back and have your daughter apologise to the owner. Have her write out the apology in a home-made card. Talk about how the other person feels when their things are stolen. Have your daughter do regular jobs so that she can earn money and appreciate the value of items.

Tantrums

41. We always seem to have a tantrum around 2 o'clock every afternoon. Why is this happening, and what can I do?

A tantrum at the same time each day can usually be related to a specific cause. In this case, as you are on one nap a day, it is probably mostly due to tiredness. Rearrange your schedule and pop your little one into bed half an hour earlier.

Tantrums

42. I was embarrassed today when my 18-month-old child screamed for 10 minutes in the supermarket when I said no to some sweets. He was so loud. Can I prevent this happening next time? (This has happened on the last five shopping trips).

Yes, you can! As a mum, you do greatly influence your child's behaviour. Within the framework of a flexible pattern you can train your child to accept a 'No'. How? By calmly and consistently providing a consequence every time they scream their response. In the privacy of your own home, 5 – 15 minutes isolation may be an option for a child of this age.

Your child's behaviour in public is a reflection of what happens in the home, and as you train your child to have self-control each day at home, your shopping trips can become a pleasure for you both.

Tantrums

43. Do you have a positive way to avoid or minimise temper tantrums?

Picture a softball diamond. To score a run in a softball game, you need to hit the ball and then run to first base, then second, then third and finally home base. A tantrum can be described as a home run on home base.

On first base, your child may display his disapproval of your decisions or instructions with his facial expression or mild words. On second base, your child may display his disapproval of your decisions or instructions with his body language (e.g. dragging his feet around, slumping his shoulders) and loud words or whining.

On third base, your child may display his disapproval of your decisions and instructions with stronger body language (stamping feet, lashing out at you, lying on the floor) and screaming and crying. At home base, your child will display his disapproval of your decisions and instructions with a temper tantrum. This can take the form of kicking, screaming, swearing, throwing objects, destroying a room, head butting, vomiting, soiling pants, extended mood, biting, high pitched whining, uncontrollable sobbing, or any combination of these.

As the parent, you can choose at which base you will train your child to obedience. If you consistently train at first or second base, then your child will rarely progress to the following bases. If you simply ignore, distract or excuse the behaviour at first or second base, then your child will probably progress to third base and then home base.

If you have allowed your child to move to home base, it is possible to move your child back, with calm and consistent training, but it will be most unpleasant for the first few weeks of this. Your child will not be willing to give up the ground he has already claimed. Focus on the long-term goals during this time, as after this initial pulling back, life will be much better for everyone for many years.

If your child is just entering the toddler age group, you can decide – at what point will you take charge? What will be the short-term and long-term consequences of your choice for your child, yourself and those around you?

Tantrums

44. My little one is fairly obedient most of the time but about once a week we have a major explosion and he can be screaming for over an hour. How can I prevent these episodes?

Evaluate your daily pattern to ensure your day is well balanced and structured. Are you too busy? Is your child too busy? Is this mostly a result of fatigue? Cut out a few activities (yours and his) for a week or two and see if that helps.

It may also be the result of too much free time. One or two periods of free play (say around 20–40 minutes each) every day are adequate for a toddler. Are you giving him too many choices? It is very easy to fall into the habit of asking our child to make countless decisions.

Outbursts like this are usually due to a build-up of tensions or frustrations. So, look for the warning signs. Some children may whine a little more before a major outburst, others may have a loud and angry tone, and others simply get bouncier and over active. By intervening with a quiet cuddle and special reading time with mum, you may help prevent the outburst even starting.

Topical Issues

45. My teen is beginning to express their views on global events and social issues. I'm finding this challenging, especially when their view differs from mine.

Meal times and car trips are ideal times to talk through ideas and responses to daily life and key issues. Model listening carefully and genuinely seeking to understand another viewpoint.

Model expressing your own opinion in a clear, rational and respectful manner. Model asking questions that gently point to the wider worldview of that position or guide towards the eventual consequences of that position or action. Model how to disagree agreeably.

Love them well as they work out their own views on key issues.

Toilet Training

46. I started toilet training my child at 18 months of age and nine months later she still has accidents every day. She can stay dry for at least an hour and always tells me after her pants are soiled! Help!

You have probably started a little too early, as you would want her to be regularly dry for 2 – 3 hours at a time before you start training. However, as you have started, do keep going.

Praise her for telling you when her pants are full and watch for her pattern. If, for example, she starts to always pass a motion after lunch then you can take her to the bathroom at that time. Read a book to her or practice her counting or ABC's to make the most of the time!

Pop her in thick towelling training pants to decrease accidents on the floor, and your frustration too. Be calm, patient and consistent and she will catch on in the next few months.

Toilet-Training

47. My 4-year-old will not initiate his toilet visits, and we are having 8 – 10 accidents a day. How can I encourage him to remember?

Simply have him sit on a chair after each accident. He sits, and doesn't play or talk for 5 minutes (use a timer). Try doubling this time every few days. Reward him for remembering, for example, five stickers then he gets a small toy. Be calm and very matter of fact. Calmly tell him that this is a skill that everyone needs to learn.

You may go back to planning regular toilet visits into your day. For example, after lunch and reading time, you will instruct your son to go to the toilet, and then move onto rest time. After a few days, you can ask your son to tell you what comes after reading time, and then gradually he can initiate the toilet visit at that time himself. Reward him for remembering.

Having a child helping to clean up after the accident is effective for some. Not only does he experience all the work and time that goes into the clean-up process, he is also losing out on playtime – much quicker simply to go to the toilet.

Verbal-Freedom

48. My eight-year-old girl constantly talks from morning to night. I get so frustrated and end up yelling at her to stop. How can I handle this in a more positive way?

Balance your routine to include times where she plays alone and times where she interacts with her siblings and parents. This will ensure she has times of quiet as well as times for talking.

Also, do encourage her to only talk to you when she has full eye contact. This can greatly reduce the yelling out to mum from another room or the other end of the house that can be so frustrating. It will also give mum a few breaks during the day, from the constant thinking and listening, and will greatly help her patience and tolerance levels.

At meal times, encourage her to share one bit of news from her day and then ask another family member to share their news of the day. This will help her see that conversation involves listening and talking. Finally, do ensure you have one or two times each day where you sit and listen to her talk and share. This is especially important at bedtime when they will often open the window to their heart.

Virtue Training

49. Wow! I was really struggling with the never-ending regularity of my daily tasks. Now I can see real value in using these as teaching opportunities. Where can I get ideas of other virtues and positive traits to teach all my children? What else can I teach my toddler?

Training your child to have a happy, healthy heart is an enjoyable and incredibly rewarding experience. It adds immense value to your daily tasks and it is such a privilege to be influencing a little life in such a special way. This teaching will also make your day very manageable.

Your toddler will bring you, and others, a lot of pleasure within the home and you will avoid a lot of embarrassment outside the home. However, the goal of virtue training should be far more than for your own convenience.

All the qualities of the heart reflect the heart of God. By teaching your precious child these attributes of God, you are laying a wonderful foundation for introducing your child to the God of love himself.

There are many other virtues you can train into the heart and life of your child. This book has only touched on a few examples. I hope it has motivated you to make the most of this crucial stage of your child's development.

The Bible is the best guidebook for all of life, including parenting. One of my favourite parts of the Bible is the middle book of the Bible called Proverbs, which is filled with practical wisdom.

Also, do enjoy teaching your toddler his academic skills, nursery rhymes, songs, verses, physical skills and personal care tasks. Toddlers are so interested in anything new and absolutely love to feel grown up by mastering tasks or knowledge. Enjoy being the primary teacher of your child during this wonderful stage of their life.

Whining

50. My three-year-old girl whines all day and I have tried everything to stop it. Can you offer me any suggestions?

First, have a medical check up to ensure there is no physical reason for this whining if it is excessive. Ensure that you are implementing a predictable and balanced pattern into your child's week. The vast majority of the whining will disappear when your child knows what is happening and when it is happening.

For example, if you have morning tea after focus play every day, then the child will not need to be asking for food all morning. If you always have a video straight after lunch, then she will not need to constantly ask for it.

Then you need to evaluate why she is whining. Is she simply copying the people around her? Some children whine in their requests for food or a video etc. Simply have her sit in a chair, set your timer for 2 or 3 minutes and then have the child ask again, nicely this time.

After a day, double the time she has to wait. I have seen some very determined whiners cured in just a week using this idea. Your child may be whining to get attention. Ensure you have a focus time with each child every day, even 10 minutes with mum is effective.

Most children, however, will whine because they do not like your instruction and this is their way of expressing that. Treat it as if she had overtly rejected your authority and apply a strong consequence. I found that 10 – 20 minutes of isolation for a whiny response was most effective. Be calm and consistent, every time.

Resources

Toddler to Teen

- Blog: www.melhayde.wordpress
  Speaking Requests and Trade Discounts: melishayde@gmail.com
  Facebook: www.Facebook.com/ToddlerToTeen

Parenting Resources

- Growing Families Australia – resources and parenting courses
  www.gfi.org.au
  Facebook: www.Facebook.com/GrowingFamiliesAustralia
- Cyber Parenting – by James and Simone Boswell
  www.cyberparentingbook.com
  Facebook: CyberParentingBook
  Speaking Requests: james@boswellbunch.com
- Calm Baby, Confident Mum – by Simone Boswell
  www.calmbabyconfidentmum.com
  Speaking Requests: simone@boswellbunch.com

- **Other Websites**
  www.angathome.com
  www.lifestyle-homeschool.com
  www.ccef.org
  www.cluonline.com

www.ingramcontent.com/pod-product-compliance
Lightning Source LLC
Chambersburg PA
CBHW071343080526
44587CB00017B/2937